three · dark · days

KENNETH MACDONALD

Highl

s

Text copyright © Kenneth MacDonald, 1999

First published in Scotland in 1999
and republished in 2006 by Acair Ltd.,
7 James Street, Stornoway,
Isle of Lewis, Scotland HS1 2QN

Tel: 01851 703020
Fax: 01851 703294
www.acairbooks.com
info@acairbooks.com

Cover design and illustration by Fiona Robson
Book design Margaret Anne Macleod
Printed by ColourBooks Ltd., Dublin

ISBN 0 86152 225 9
EAN 9 780861 522252

three · dark · days

KENNETH MACDONALD

acair

This book is dedicated to the memory of my dear brother, Donald Calum Macdonald, who first sent this manuscript to the publisher.

Calum! Cove, I miss you, like the flowers miss the rain; like the trees forget to blossom at the height of summer time. Man, I miss you like a mountain on the empty plain of life; like an evening turned to darkness with no coming of the dawn. Your leaving left a vacuum that's impossible to fill; that no end of pain or grief can justify.

But, dammit, Cove, I'll find you, when my time is set to go, and we'll sail the tranquil, silver oceans of the sky.

To the fond memory of my father, who taught me the hard way, how to sail.

Also to the memory of Kim. A true companion and constant friend.

1

This book is about a young British merchant seaman, who was like all others of his age, full of vigour and bursting with self confidence, as if the world belonged to them, which in a manner of speaking, it did. They sailed across one ocean after another, to one foreign port after another, with nothing on their minds after months at sea but the first bar or knock-shop outside the dock gate. All with the same conviction, of the old saying, that the three best things in life are the drink before and the cigarette afterwards.

I bumbled along like this for a while, until I realised that there was more to it when people would ask me, "What was this country like?" or "What was that country like?" I felt a bit of a clown when I couldn't tell them, although I could tell them all the different brands of beer and the number of doors on the bars round the docks.

So any time after that when I was in a foreign port I would jump on a bus and give the driver the equivalent of twenty five pence and tell him to put me off when the fare ran out. It was funny, because all the bus drivers were the same. They didn't want to let me off the bus. They would tell me to stay on the bus at no extra charge and go round their route with them, while they gave a running commentary on everything from the state of the roads, other drivers, politics and America.

When they would stop for their break it was always the same. Loud chuckling and glances towards me, as they were telling the other drivers about the daft foreigner they were taking sightseeing. When I managed to convince some of them that I really did want to get off the bus, I would make my way on foot back to the docks.

At the weekends I would find the nearest railway station, and with my haversack I would take a train and see how far I could get inland from the docks for a pound. Sometimes it would be in the early hours of Monday morning before I arrived back at my ship, having slept rough for a couple of nights.

It opened up a whole new world for me. I would meet a lot of interesting people and see some amazing sights. It gave me a freedom that was unbelievable, being able to walk for hours on end after being cooped aboard the ship, where you could only walk for a few yards without going over the side or colliding with a winch or bulkhead.

When I would be walking back to my ship at the weekends, I would walk through small villages and towns where the people would offer me food and water, and look at me as if I was mad when I refused the many offers of lifts from trucks, vans, tractors, cars and carts.

The only problem I had when I went on my excursions was the number of stray dogs, of various colours and varieties, that used to follow me. One bunch would follow me for about two to three miles until they met up with another lot, which without fail would develop into a snarling session until the first lot turned and went back. Then the new lot would follow me. It seemed as if they were working some kind of relay to escort me out of their territory.

I even arrived back at the ship one time with four dogs following me to the bottom of the gangway, to the merriment of the crew who started calling me 'Bow, wow'.

On my walks I would see strange trees and plants, animals, birds, insects and reptiles of all descriptions, and I met a lot of kind, friendly people who couldn't do enough to help me when I would try and ask for directions.

2

My first recollection of the pain of sail was as a nine or ten year old boy out fishing with my father.

When we had finished baiting and setting our lobster pots he hauled up our patched lug-sail and headed for home. We were about halfway home when he started to tie the lobster claws, so as they wouldn't be able to fight each other in the keep. He held the tiller under his arm and told me to hold the lug-sheet while he used both hands to tie a lobster's claws, which he held between his knees.

As I held on to the lug-sheet a gust of wind slightly stronger than the rest hit the sail and tore the rope out of my hands, along with most of the skin from my palms and fingers. Seeming unconcerned, he turned the boat into the wind and with the sail flapping, he asked me why I had let go the sheet. When I told him that it had hurt my hands, he asked to see them. And as I showed him my bleeding hands he said, "That's nothing. We will soon sort that."

He pulled over the bait barrel, which was an alloy beer barrel that had the top removed, with a buoy cut in half as a lid to keep the water out. Our bait was mackerel, which we caught ourselves over the summer months with hand lines and salted down in barrels with rough rock-salt to preserve them over the winter. It was the most enjoyable task imaginable on those long hot summer days, to get stuck in a big shoal of mackerel with six hooks on your hand-line and to watch your boxes fill up.

When he took the cover off the bait barrel, the mackerel was floating about in a thick mixture of dense salt brine and fish oil. Grabbing both my hands, he plunged them into the mushy bree and held them there until the pain from the salt made my knee-joints ache.

After that he just reset the sail and carried on home. When we got ashore and he had finished pulling the boat out on her running mooring, he took a bar of McCowan's Highland toffee out of his pocket and gave it to me. In my childish innocence I asked him why he hadn't given it to me out in the boat, and he said, "If I had given it to you then you wouldn't have it now." I didn't really understand what he meant, so I thought it would be better if I just stayed quiet and ate the toffee before he changed his mind.

The strange thing is that my hands, after being dipped in the mackerel oil and bree, healed up completely after two days.

3

It was a gentle spring day in the Islands and one of those rare calm late afternoon silences which doesn't happen very often.

The only snag was that the silence was being broken at regular intervals by the rasp and buzz of a chain-saw, which was coming from a stand of large spruce trees a short distance from the road, where a small van was parked. On the other side of the van, a white-haired middle-aged man was in the process of finishing off trimming a wind-blown tree, which had been blocking a foot-path, through the stand of timber.

Each time the razor-sharp chain of the saw touched, a branch of the tree fell to the ground, and he kicked it out of the way with his boot. On he went methodically, cut clear, cut clear, until the last branch fell to the ground. The tree lying on the ground, stripped of its branches, straight and clean, would have made a good mast for any boat.

Straightening his back, to get the kinks out of it, he switches off his saw and looks around him. Then he picks up the plastic chain-protector and slips it over the bar of the chain-saw. He then walks down to the butt end of the tree and sits down on the freshly cut stump, placing the saw on the ground beside him. Taking out his watch, he checks the time. Ten minutes to knocking-off.

He takes out his tobacco pouch and starts to roll a cigarette, thinking to himself, "I shouldn't really ... the wife keeps on to me about my smoking." Lighting his cigarette, he starts wondering how long he has been married. Twenty-seven, twenty-eight years, he can't remember. He doesn't think that a full waking hour has passed, in the years since he met her, that she hasn't crossed his mind for some reason or other. It's more like a haunting than anything else. Taking a draw on his cigarette and expelling the smoke slowly, he turns round to look at a small burn that runs alongside the path which ends in quite a large pool. How Kim used to love it here, he thinks. She would splash about in the water all day while he would be working on the trees. How she loved to play in the water.

Kim was his dog, a German Shepherd bitch which he got as a small puppy, and they were inseparable for eight years. Until she contacted a form of glandular virus, which the vets couldn't do anything to cure, after trying all they could think of, and all that was possible.

The emptiness and grief at the loss of his dog triggered off in his mind memories that had been buried deep and forgotten about, for over thirty years.

They were memories of an incident which happened some time before he met his wife. Memories that he had never mentioned to a living soul - not even to those closest to him - all of which had been completely forgotten until the trauma of losing his dog had taken them back from the depth of his mind with a startling clarity. So intense were the memories after all those years that he would try and put off going to sleep for as long as possible because of the dreams and recurring nightmares.

4

I try to write this as it was told to me over a period of three long dark days and three long nights, in a mixture of English, some words of French, and mime. But mostly in drawings and diagrams with charcoal sticks on the deck.

The names I am writing down as they sounded to me, as I couldn't even begin to spell them right, or pronounce them. I have a very rough idea of the area this is about, but the names of the villages, rivers and roads, I just can't remember.

In the second half of the sixties in South East Asia at the very southern tip of Vietnam, thirty to forty miles from the Cambodian border, and about ten to fifteen miles from the coast, there was quite a large village.

At the centre of the village was a factory belonging to a man called Luc. Thirteen years before this, he had started a business making glass bowls and cups in a small hut. His life consisted of working long hours and re-investing all the profits and spare cash back into the business.

Over the years he reached a stage where he now employed fourteen workers in a big building. They operated three furnaces for melting different types of sand to make glass. Now they produced all kinds of glass products, drinking glasses, glass for windows in houses, trucks and all types of vehicles.

Luc was a very worried man as he worked away in the late afternoon, grading the sand for tomorrow's smelt in the furnace. He kept thinking of the rumours he had been hearing during the last three weeks. About intimidation, beatings and two murders in the villages to the north and east of his village, by groups of three or four men dressed in black loose-fitting clothes.

They travel around the countryside from village to village demanding that the villagers follow them. And as a token of loyalty, they beat up the bosses and employers, who they maintain to be suppressors of the people and parasites on all communities.

What bothered him most was hearing of two beatings and a house-burning in his own village last night.

Working steadily, weighing the different grades of sand, he glanced up and spotted two black-clothed men talking to his workers at the other end of the building, going to each one, pausing for a short time to talk, then moving on to the next one. Dropping his scales, he decides to go and talk to them and starts weaving his way through the boxes of packed glass. He reaches about halfway down the building when they stop talking and turn to stare at him. Without saying a word, they both turn around and walk quickly through the outside door.

When Luc reached the door and looked out he was surprised to see that there was nobody on the street anywhere near his building, as if nobody wanted to be seen near himself or his building.

He went back inside the factory and looked for his brother-in-law, Poi.

Poi had married Luc's sister four years ago. When he saw him by one of the furnaces, which he was repairing, Luc started making his way through the packing cases towards him. When Poi looked up and checked to see if anyone was watching, he then signalled for Luc to go behind the furnace.

After a minute or two Poi worked his way round to the back of the furnace to where Luc stood, out of sight and out of hearing of the other workers. Before Luc could say a word, Poi turned and said to him, "My brother in all but birth, I fear that we are finished. You no doubt have been wondering where I have been the last two nights instead of working late with you as we always do. Listen to me, for I tell the truth. We are in grave danger. I have travelled far in the last two nights, listening to the huddled whispering at the meeting places and the loud bragging in the drinking dens, and they all say the same.

"There are strangers amongst us from the north, who are dressed in the same clothes as us. The two in black who were here today are generals in the North Vietnamese army. They only appear in public when they

11

have a large number of their own soldiers in civilian clothes infiltrated among the people.

"Those who show any signs of disagreeing with them and who refuse to listen to their speeches are immediately picked out from the crowd by the henchmen and beaten with short lengths of bamboo, which they keep hidden underneath their jackets, as a warning to the rest.

"Closer to home, the danger is here. Our own workers have turned against us to follow the generals. Some follow for their beliefs, others because of the terror and threats that have been made against them. Others! The ones who brag and shout in the drinking dens, those are the ones that I fear most. They have been promised your factory and the business you have worked so hard to build over the years.

"But first, my dear brother, they have been told to kill you. And I am to be beaten up so severely that I will not be able to work again, and left a beggar on the streets, as a token of their allegiance and commitment to the generals and their cause. The blind fools, if they kill you they will not be able to run the factory, as you are the only one who knows the sand mixtures for the different types of glass. But that is not the way they think. Our lives are counted not in days but in hours."

Poi paused for a drink of water. Luc, who by now was stunned, said, "We must make plans immediately and get our families to safety away from this madness."

When Poi finished his drink he said to Luc, "Fear not my brother, I have been planning for the last two days. Even as we speak now my wife and family are waiting ready to go tonight, and you and yours must come with us. I have made plans for us to cross the border into Cambodia to our friends with whom we have been doing business over the years. We have to leave everything and only take what we can carry on our backs in haversacks and packs.

"For the last two days my wife and our mother have been going round the markets buying food, no more than a day's supply of rice and dried food at each stall, so as not to arouse suspicion. They have gathered enough to last our two families ten days, for a journey that should only take six days if everything goes well."

Luc, who was by now sitting on the dusty floor, said, "Poi, my brother, as always you are right. I have been concentrating and putting more effort into my work to try and forget what is happening all around me. Like the bird that buries its head in the sand and hopes that it will all go away. We will load our belongings into our old pick-up truck and make the journey in two days."

"No!" said Poi. "We will leave the pick-up, as it is too well-known throughout the area. We must walk and join the others who are fleeing from the north, more and more as each day goes by. With them we will be one amongst many, and harder for those who seek us to find us when they realise we have fled. I have arranged all except one thing. You must go to your home and gather all your gold and silver ornaments and trinkets, as we have with ours. You must then take them back here when all the workers have left and we will melt them down on the furnace, moulding them into small ingots which will be easier to carry and conceal.

"We will then stoke the furnaces, banking them down as always, ready for tomorrow's work. So if they come looking for us here and see that the furnaces are banked, hopefully they should think that we will be back in the morning. This will give us an extra hour or two to prepare.

"We will be going to the south-west. But before this, I will take the pick-up and load some of our best, smaller bits of furniture on to it and drive a short distance to the north-west before abandoning it. When it's found, with a bit of luck the morons will think that we have fled to the north-west. Our furniture, which we are going to lose anyway, will buy us some time. When they come to our homes they will steal and destroy everything, and like animals defecate in our homes. No! not like animals. Worse. Animals never dirty in their own nests.

"When we leave we will leave the fires on, food ready to eat, lights on and the doors unlocked, to give the impression that we aren't far away and will be returning soon. By the time they have destroyed our homes and realise that we have gone, we should be well on our way to the border."

Luc and Poi slip out the side door beside the furnace, go to their battered old pick-up, and set off to their homes which are beside each other. On their way, Luc tells Poi that he is sad to leave after all those years, "We have made well in the years of peace. But that is over. Now all is changing and the cruelty is starting all over again. Those in power aren't happy with their power, and those who aren't in power aren't happy with those in power. I fear our beautiful country will be turned into a battlefield to please the ignorant beliefs of others, who will use them to further their own profits and positions. It is the poor blind fools who follow them and listen to their long speeches who will suffer. And those who don't care, who just want to get on with their lives, they will suffer the most. I have a terrible feeling of foreboding.

"We will be able to travel only at night, and be well hidden in the trees before the sun comes up. My poor wife will be shocked when I tell her that we have to leave at once, our home and all that is dear to her to be left behind."

Poi, who was driving, said, "No Luc, my wife and our mother have been with her all day preparing. Even as we speak she will be waiting with our ornaments and trinkets in two bags for us to collect and melt down. All except her wedding band which she will wear round her neck on a string, because there have been stories of women having their fingers cut off by bandits if their rings are difficult to remove.

"My only worry is your sister, my wife, who as you know is due to give birth in four weeks' time. But being a strong and determined woman she doesn't want to stay where her own life and her baby's life will be in danger from the turmoil that is sweeping through our land.

"I am sorry that I kept our plans from you, but we wanted to be sure before telling you. Sure that you were with us in your thinking. Sure that the rumours were not just rumours. As I have found out, the situation is far worse than the rumours suggested."

After a pause Luc said, "You have done well and planned well. I will follow with mine and do as you say. You were always the far thinker. At work you could spot the cause of an accident before it happened."

The pick-up drew up beside Luc's house, and when they got out Luc saw that both families were together, dressed in heavy clothes. There were a number of bulging haversacks and packs spread on the floor.

His mother and his wife said, "We are ready to go, all is prepared," and handing him two medium-sized sacks said, "Here are the sacks with our treasures. Take them and do as you must, but hurry!"

Luc noticed his wife's and the other women's bare fingers, but didn't like to say anything.

Taking the sacks and giving one of them to Poi, they both go out to the pick-up and set off to the factory.

Before they arrive at the factory they notice a number of their workers dodging down the alleyways, obviously having spotted the pick-up coming, and not wanting to be seen. When they reach the factory, they go into a silent deserted workplace. All the employees have left.

Poi said to Luc, "Hurry! As I have feared, it has started. We have little time left. They will be gathering their courage out of bottles and bragging to each other with brave words."

Luc worked feverishly at the furnace, while Poi stoked the others and banked them down for the morning. Finishing, Luc banked down his furnace and picked up three small square tins shouting at Poi to come. They both go out of the factory through the side door, leaving the lights on, and drive away in the pick-up.

Arriving back at their homes in the dusk, they eat some of the food that is to be left on the table, and make sure that the children who have been sleeping all day have been fed. They start loading the pick-up with the smaller bits of furniture, telling all to hurry and to put their haversacks and packs on, as by now darkness has fallen and it is time to go, because as each minute passes, the danger increases.

Poi told them to follow the back path through the trees to the place where the roads meet, and to hide in the trees beside the road until he gets back. His wife knows the way, so she will guide them.

Before they leave, Poi goes to the shed and appears with a goat on the end of a rope. He gives it to Luc and says, "We need it for milk for the children and my wife. Now go!"

He watches them disappearing into the darkness. Without hesitating he turns back into the shed and wheels out a bicycle. Lifting it into the back of the pick-up he covers it with an old piece of tarpaulin, starts the engine and drives round the back streets until he joins the main road which runs in a north westerly direction from his village. Driving steadily over pot-holes and ruts until he is about two miles from the village, he pulls into the side of the road, stops the engine and lifts the bonnet. Taking out his knife he scrapes at the fan belt until it frays apart without leaving a clean cut. He then drains the water out of the engine and closes the drain tap, puts the frayed fan belt in his pocket, starts the engine and leaves it running, knowing that without water it will overheat and stop, hopefully seizing up. Going round the back, he lifts his bicycle out and scatters the furniture in the back, throwing a few pieces on to the side of the road to make it look as if whoever was in the pick-up left in a hurry when it broke down, taking with them only what they could carry, having to abandon the rest.

Pedalling his bike back the way he came, trying to avoid the pot-holes in the dark, he covers about two hundred yards. He takes the frayed fan belt out of his pocket and drops it in the middle of the road, where it will be easily spotted, convincing whoever finds it of the reason for the pick-up being abandoned.

Pedalling on with as much haste as the dark and pot-holes allow, he arrives at the outskirts of his village and decides to go round the back streets to save time. Pedalling behind the buildings in front of the square, where the market is held, he hears screams and shouting. Leaving his bicycle propped beside a building, he walks carefully up a narrow alleyway between two buildings that leads into the market place. As he comes round the corner he can see a crowd of about twenty to thirty people shouting and laughing. Some of them have lengths of bamboo, about four to five foot long, and seem to be hitting the ground with them.

Stepping into the shadow of a doorway, so as not to be seen, he wonders what the screams were that he had been hearing before. Then the crowd moves back and on the ground he can see the bodies of two naked people.

He recognises them as the salt merchant and his wife who live in a big house not far from the centre of the village. They are covered in blood and moaning pitifully. He can remember the wife at the markets, all dressed in fancy clothes. She would have her two maids in tow, and they did the bartering for the goods, as speaking to the stall-holders was beneath her. Even so, the poor woman didn't deserve this. Two people leave the crowd and fill a bucket of water, each with a pump, from a trough in the centre of the square.

Laughing and gesturing to the rest of the crowd, they empty the buckets of water over the two tormented people on the ground to revive them. As they struggle to get up and try to escape, the mob move in with their sticks and the screaming starts again.

Horrified, Poi moves quickly round the corner and back down the alleyway. He is thinking of the poor salt merchant, whom he knew to be a kind and fair man who never under-weighted his salt or over-charged the people, always giving a little bit extra, for, as he would say, settlement.

The madness had started.

"I have to get back to the rest and pray that we haven't left it too late." Jumping on to his bicycle he cycles through the village as fast as he can, trying to keep out of sight and avoiding lit-up areas until he comes to the start of the path through the trees where he had seen the rest disappearing into the darkness before he left with the pick-up. Not being able to see where he was going after leaving the lights of the village, he fell off the bicycle once, and collided with a tree on another occasion. This made him decide to run, pushing the bicycle to make better time. The worry and panic was building up inside him, giving strength to his legs and making him ignore the sweat which was running down into his eyes, blinding him. Stumbling off the path, through some undergrowth, he sprawled on to the road and rode his bicycle towards the cross-roads two miles away. He hoped the rest would be waiting, safely hidden for his return.

He had cycled about a mile and a half when he noticed the lights of a vehicle in the distance, coming up behind him. Leaping off his bicycle, he hid himself and the bicycle in the undergrowth at the side of the road and waited for the vehicle to pass.

As it came closer it started slowing down and stopped about four hundred yards back from his hiding place. Knowing he hadn't been seen, he decided to creep along the ditch beside the road to have a look.

When he gets closer, he can see that it is a military lorry with at least a dozen soldiers, dressed in different uniforms. They are setting up a road-block with posts and barbed wire. Guiding the operation with shouts and commands are three dressed in the black of the North Vietnamese army. Shuddering at his narrow escape, he gives thanks to his forethought in deciding to flee to safety with their families before the roads were closed. He creeps back along the ditch to his bicycle, praying that the others are waiting safely for him, and pedals desperately towards the cross-roads away from the road-block. In what seems a matter of minutes he arrives at the cross-roads. Standing beside his bicycle, he is not sure where to start looking for the rest in the dark. He decides to give a low whistle, which is answered from the undergrowth to his left. As he moves towards the answering whistle a dark form appears silently beside him.

Before he can say a word, Luc is speaking out of the darkness and hugging him at the same time. He says, "My brother, we were worried. You were away so long and are so tired. Have some water and food, for we must travel another three hours to the south and be settled down safe and well hidden before the first fingers of grey come into the sky."

Moving to the side of the road where the rest have gathered after coming out of the trees, he eats some food and in between mouthfuls tells them about the road-block and the cruelty he has seen in the village by the mobs, which included some of their own workers and friends.

While Poi eats his food and rests, Luc is making sure that their packs are secure and that they haven't left anything behind that will attract attention to their hiding place. He tells Poi to rest for a few more minutes. Having the bicycle, he will soon catch up with them. He then gets everyone walking along the road. Leading the goat by the rope, he says to his wife, "I was never one for the land and animals!"

Poi, who has now rested for some time, starts riding his bicycle after them and soon catches up. Luc tells him to go on ahead for some distance to make sure the road is clear, and to wait until the rest catch up. If there is any danger, he is to ride back and warn them to give them time to get off the road into hiding.

As the hours go by, the fourth time they catch up with Poi they can see him a short distance away; a sign of the coming dawn. Moving off together they start looking for a place to hide before daybreak. About a hundred yards down the road they go into a clump of trees beside the earth embankment of a disused rice field.

Milking the goat, and mixing the milk with cooked rice and water from the rice fields, they eat silently, each one with their own thoughts of home and of friends they'd left behind and of the journey to the border ahead. Finishing eating, they settle down to sleep, exhausted after the rush and tension of the night's flight.

The day passes, and as the night closes in they prepare to leave. Filling all the containers with water and checking for anything left behind, they start walking in the darkness once again.

On they go for another two nights. Poi was back and fore with his bicycle, keeping watch. On the third night, as they were looking for a place to hide, they came on to the main highway going to the south-west. Hiding in the undergrowth a short distance away from the road, they prepared to settle down for the day. By the time they finished their food, the sun had risen above the horizon and they start to prepare shelters with leaves and branches for shade. They hear voices and movement in the trees around them. Going to investigate, Luc can see two different groups like themselves, who obviously have been resting through the night and are preparing to travel. Watching them for some time, they move out of the trees on to the road and follow it to the south-west. Looking to the north-east Luc can see others who have rested overnight coming along the road, all at the same pace, steadily moving to the south-west.

Returning to the rest, he tells them what he has seen

and they decide amongst themselves to stay and sleep for a while, taking turns on lookout, to enable them to recover from the night's travelling.

It was mid-afternoon by the time they had recovered enough to start off again. Luc took his group down to the road first. Poi waited until they had put a distance of three to four hundred yards between them. He then moved down to the road and followed with his group, holding back to keep a steady distance between the two groups.

He had tied the packs belonging to the elderly and the children on to both sides of his bicycle and was pushing it along, trying to keep away from the others travelling in the same direction, so as to avoid making conversation.

As darkness started to fall, the other people slowed down and wandered off the road in groups towards the trees to find shelter and settle for the night.

In the distance he noticed that Luc and his group had left the road and were walking towards a large clump of trees and undergrowth where he would join them to rest for the remainder of the long evening.

Before he reached the place where Luc had left the road, a large military lorry, travelling at speed, roared past, going in the same direction, scattering all. As it passed him in a flurry of dust, he could see into the back of it, and saw that it was full of soldiers.

This worried Poi, when he started thinking back to the night he had so narrowly missed the road-block they had put up behind him. He spots Luc waving to him and hurries his group as they make their way into the trees.

Joining with the rest, they have some food and prepare to stay for the night. Luc tells him that he has spoken to those on the road, who all said that the news to the north and west was the same; killing, beating and burning of whole villages, shooting anybody who showed the slightest doubt or protest. A number also said that a day and a half's walk will take them to a main bridge which is only seven miles from the border.

Bedding down for the night, Poi's wife said to him that she was worried for the old ones. "Our mother and your father; they keep talking about the wars with the French, and seem to be getting very low in spirit at times," she told him.

Poi said to her, "It is best to ignore their talk. They know, as the rest of us do, that we have no option left to us except to go on."

For two days they walked, with more people joining the main road at each junction. There was a steady unbroken stream of people crowding the road. Some were pushing prams and hand carts, and oxen were pulling carts with all their belongings. But mostly they had poles on their shoulders, with packs at each end, balancing them. There was also a large number pushing bicycles loaded down with cases and packs.

On the morning of the third day, word swept back through the crowds that the bridge was only a mile away.

Poi, still thinking of the army lorry with the soldiers that had passed, said to Luc, "We will go half way and hide in the trees until the afternoon. Then I will go to the bridge with my bicycle to make sure all is well."

In the afternoon Poi set off pushing his bicycle, still with the packs tied to it, so as not to be conspicuous and to blend in with the others. He was about halfway to the bridge, which was at the end of a curve in the road, when he heard shots. Pushing his bicycle off the road into the trees, he hid it and walked through the trees until he had a clear view of the bridge from the side of the river.

The army lorry that had passed some days before is parked at the side of the road and the soldiers have set up a road-block.

On the embankment at the end of the bridge there is a dead ox, with its cart broken and scattered round it. Its contents are lying on the ground, where they fell. He thinks the ox must have broken a leg and that the shots he heard were the soldiers shooting it to clear the road. Deciding to have a closer look, he goes back to his bicycle and pushes it on to the road where he joins up with the rest of the people, who are moving slowly towards the far end of the bridge.

As he watches, the soldiers are searching bags and packs. Anything of value to them is put into the back of the lorry and the packs thrown on to the ground, to be picked up by the owner, who is then allowed to continue.

As a soldier grabbed another pack to open it, the man

held back for a moment and was shot immediately by another soldier. He then rolls the body down the embankment on the opposite side of the road to the dead ox, where Poi could see a number of bodies in the bottom of the ditch.

Instantly he loosened one of the packs on the bicycle and let it drop to the road. He carried on until one of the people behind him shouted, as he had hoped, to tell him that he had lost one of his packs. Slowly he turned his bicycle round and went back to where the pack lay on the ground. Picking it up, he wasted time trying to tie it back on to his bicycle, until the soldiers' view was blocked by the other people. Then he pushed the bicycle back along the road to where the rest were hiding.

Arriving exhausted, he told Luc about the murders and robberies he saw and that there was no hope of them safely crossing the river by the bridge. But the way to go was to follow the river down from the place where he first saw the bridge. They should leave now, while the others were still travelling on the road, and follow the river until dusk and rest for the night.

When they reached the spot where Poi turned off the road, they walked through the trees to the river, staying hidden from those on the bridge and the soldiers on the other side, who they could see through the foliage.

As they watch the steady stream of refugees being systematically robbed by the so-called soldiers, a woman hesitates, trying to hold on to a bag which a soldier is pulling from her. A man beside her, whom they think is her husband, tries to take the bag from her to give to the soldier. Before he can get her to release the bag, the soldier steps back and shoots both of them, and rolls their bodies with his foot over the embankment. He then kicks the bag, without bothering to open it, after them.

Silently they move away, following a very narrow path which runs alongside the river, until it turns slightly inland through a shallow marsh which reaches up to their knees, making walking difficult.

Poi and Luc have moved out ahead, searching disused huts and buildings for a boat or anything which they could use to cross the river.

Coming out of the marsh before darkness, they prepare to rest for the night. They light a small fire to dry their clothes and cook the first hot food since leaving home.

In the morning as they prepare to leave, one of the children runs up to Poi's wife and says to her, "Our old mother won't wake up for us." When they go over to the place where she was sleeping, they find that she has died peacefully in her sleep. The strain of the last few days has been too much for her. The old man walks slowly over and touches her body three times with a short length of stick which he has been carrying with him all the time. He then leaves to sit down a short distance away, taking no further interest in anything.

Poi and Luc take their mother's body to the edge of the

tree line and dig a grave in the soft soil with sharpened sticks. When Luc says, "It is deep enough," they lower her body down and fill the grave back in with their hands.

Luc, on his knees beside his mother's grave, curses his father, whether he be dead or alive, for abandoning her when they were small, and leaving her to a life of poverty and hardship, struggling to bring up two small children alone, with nothing. Still kneeling, he promises his dead mother that he will protect the rest and get them to safety.

Rising up, he says, "Now we go. We have to cross the river today, as two days' walk from here we will be at the coast."

Gathering everybody, they start to leave. Then Poi turns back and pulls up four thorn bushes by the roots from the side of the tree line. He carries them over to where they have buried his mother-in-law and plants them neatly on top of the grave.

When Luc asks him, "Why?" he replies, "The sharp thorns will stop people or animals walking or trampling over our mother's grave." Luc says to him, "As always, you are the far thinker."

Moving on, following the path alongside the river, with still no means of crossing it, they quietly pass a number of inhabited areas of two or three huts built on stilts, which they can see through the trees. They know this is a positive sign that the river floods the low-lying areas during the heavy rains.

About two hours before darkness, still following the

path, Poi who is ahead pushing his bicycle, tangles up in a length of fishing line. As he tries to clear it away from the bicycle pedals, a bang sounds close beside him in the trees, like a shot, but not quite so loud. He signals to the rest to pass and hide in the trees further along the path. As he clears the pedals, Luc, who has stayed to help, realises that the fishing line is going into the river and the other end is connected to a device in the trees. The device looks like a bird-scarer, which fires when a fish takes the bait.

Hearing voices and shouting coming from the trees, Luc tells Poi to go and hide along the path with the rest. Watching from the trees, Poi can barely contain his anger when Luc entangles the fishing line round his prized goat's foreleg, and runs up the path towards them, leaving the goat struggling to free itself.

As they watch from their hiding place, they see four armed men laughing and joking as they move through the trees with guns hanging over their shoulders by the slings, obviously not expecting trouble. As they come closer to the goat, the laughter becomes louder.

Two of them catch the goat and free it from the line. The third one, who seems to be the leader, unslings his gun which is a machine-gun with a long curved magazine. The others are armed with shotguns and a sporting rifle. He points his machine-gun at the goat, intending to shoot it, until one of the other men shouted, "No!" and says, "If we shoot it here we will have to carry it back. We will make it walk back and shoot it at the camp." Nodding, he slings the gun over his shoulder and says to the fourth man, who is re-baiting hooks on the fishing line, "Bait well, our powerful fisherman, who sets his hooks in a river and catches a goat."

As the four move off through the trees, dragging the goat behind them, Luc and Poi can hear them mocking the fisherman, who had reset the alarm.

They tease him, "A powerful fisherman like you should set his hooks on the land for a better chance to catch a fish for us to eat."

They waited in hiding for a time to make sure that the bandits had gone back to their camp. Luc and Poi quietly gathered the others and prepared to set off. When they were sure all was clear they moved silently, following the river which had grown far wider from bank to bank. Luc, commenting on the distance said, "We will have much further to row or paddle when we get a boat." Poi answered, "No, my brother who gave my good goat to the bandits - a prized goat that kept us in milk. But with your swift thinking, you saved us from being robbed, or at the worst, being killed. If you look at the water you will see that the flow has slowed down, a sign that we are getting nearer to the coast and the tides are affecting the river. In a number of hours from now the tide will turn and the level of the river will drop, making it much narrower at low tide. We will continue to the coast and if need be pay a fisherman to take us along the coast into Cambodia."

They leave the path once again and settle down for the night. They spent the night undisturbed. They start walking early the next day, and after travelling for about two miles, they hear the sound of an engine close by. Poi tells them to hide in the bushes by the path. He removes the packs from his bicycle and hides them beside the path, and sets off to scout out the path ahead, which turns away from the river.

Poi travels about half a mile, when the path joins on to the main coast road. The road is full of people walking along it towards the river carrying and pushing their belongings; the same as on the road to the bridge they had left. Leaving his bicycle he cuts through the trees and scrub toward the river.

From the top of a small hill he could see a compound on the far side of the river, which had been used by plantation owners to store their bales of rubber awaiting collection by boat. At one end of the compound a wooden pier jutted out into the river. Tied alongside was a boat of about thirty five feet in length. A rope of approximately two inches in diameter dropped into the water from the stern, and appeared to cross the river, connecting to a wooden pier below him. The coast road came to a stop at this pier. In a clearing beside the river there were a number of people waiting with their bags and belongings.

Poi realised that he was at a ferry. He went back through the trees to his bicycle, and with mounting excitement he pedalled back to tell the others the good news.

When he was back at their hiding place he explained what he had seen. They all seemed very happy, except his wife. She told him to calm down and to remember what had happened at the bridge. Hearing his sister speak, Luc said, "Looking ahead has kept us safe until now. We must not lower our guard. We are too near to be careless. We will go to Poi's hill and watch how things are happening on the river. When we are sure, we will go down and join the rest on the ferry."

Concealed on the hillside, they watch the ferry leave the other side.

It was guided by the two-inch rope which ran through two large metal rings in the starboard gunnel, one forward and one aft. This enabled one man who sat in the stern to control the direction of the boat. The rudder was lashed amidships. The engine would be 'astern' to come across the river and 'ahead' to go back over.

When the ferry left the far side, they could see a man with a rifle standing guard over the ferryman. Another person seemed to be sitting on the deck on the port side with a number of baskets round him.

When the ferry arrived at the pier below them, about twenty five people were taken aboard. Then the ferry set off 'ahead', crossing the river on the rope. They could make out the guard threatening the passengers if they went near either the person sitting on the deck or the ferryman.

As the ferry reached the other side, a group of armed men, some in uniform and obviously drunk, appeared out of the single building in the compound. They started shouting commands to the passengers as they left the ferry. Two armed men, one in black clothes, joined the guard on the ferry. As it set off 'astern' back across the river, one of the guards kicked the ferryman, sending him sprawling across the deck.

As the ferry made its way across, Luc and Poi could see the soldiers on the other side herding the people who had come off the ferry, with rifle butts and bayonets. They were taking them to the end of the compound beside the building. They were made to leave their packs and belongings before being herded to the back of the building, out of sight from the pier.

The ferry reached the pier below them and about thirty to forty people boarded, which was all that was left waiting to cross. It set off 'astern' again.

The ferry had reached about halfway when the soldiers went in among the passengers. They selected five of the most elderly people and pushed them over the side of the ferry into the river. Luc and Poi saw three of them surface a short distance downstream from the ferry. Immediately they were used as targets by the two soldiers with automatic rifles. Those were the ones who had come aboard after the first trip, and were drinking steadily out of wicker-covered bottles.

By now the ferry had reached the other side. The

screaming of those who had crossed over first could be heard quite clearly across the water. Watching horrified, they saw the second lot of people from the ferry being driven up to the building in the compound, with blows from rifle butts. One woman fell after being struck by a rifle, and she was then stabbed with a bayonet. On the ferry, the guard who was left picked up a basket from beside the person who was left sitting on the deck. He had not moved from that spot during both crossings of the ferry.

The guard seemed to give the person on the deck a contemptuous look as he carried the basket ashore to where about thirty armed men were gathered. They were drinking and smoking, and laughing at the terrified people in the compound.

The guard placed the basket on a bench at the end of the building. Then the others who were not already smoking picked cigarettes out of it. They lit them and inhaled deeply, coughing and nodding to each other.

Luc, who was by now dumbfounded, said to Poi, "I fear the worst. They are not soldiers but bandits and deserters who have taken over the compound and the ferry, so as to rob the travellers. Those baskets are full of narcotic cigarettes which will make them lose all their rational thinking and control."

It was not long before Luc was proven right.

The bandits started to line up the people in the compound and picking out a number of them, took them to the far end of the compound, where they began pairing them off. Drinking heavily and smoking, they started betting amongst themselves. They were using paper money and small ornaments that they had looted from the people in the compound.

Poi had been watching the guard on the pier above the ferry. He then saw the ferryman fill a bowl with water and go to the person who was still sitting on the deck. He held his head gently and put the bowl to his mouth so as he could get a drink. The guard, who had been watching the mounting excitement in the compound, turned and saw what the ferryman was doing.

He shouted at the ferryman and jumped aboard the ferry. He knocked the bowl away and kicked the ferryman at the same time, knocking him to the deck. He then stamped on the water bowl, breaking it. With the butt of his rifle he hit the ferryman three or four blows on the chest, leaving him unmoving on the deck.

Without a second glance back at the result of his handiwork, he climbed back on to the pier and continued to watch the cruelty developing in the compound.

By now the prisoners had been paired off by the bandits. They had been drinking and smoking all day and were staggering and laughing under the influence of liquor and narcotic cigarettes.

They now picked two men and made them run, racing each other, to a line at the far end of the compound. They ran half-heartedly towards the line, where about a dozen bandits stood shouting encouragement. As the first runner crossed the line some of the bandits laughed, waving money around, having won their bets. When the second prisoner crossed the line he was taken to the edge of the compound and shot. His body slumped beside the wire fence. All had to win. The second race took place and the same thing happened. The winners of these first two races could be seen collecting their packs and being allowed to walk free through a hole in the compound fence.

In the races that followed some of the runners made sure they crossed the line together. The bandits began arguing among themselves because there were too many draws amongst the runners. One of them then produced what appeared to be a wire-cutter, and they held down the next two runners. They cut off the outside toes on both their feet, and then forced them to run. The rules were then changed. Whoever dropped to the ground first was shot and the other set free, hobbling out of the compound to collapse in the trees when out of sight.

As the evening approached the bandits began to lose interest in their 'sport'. Gradually they made their way back to the building, seeming to lose all interest in the people in the compound. These then started escaping through holes in the fence. Two or three of the brave ones ran to the pile of packs and started throwing them over the wire to those on the other side, before escaping.

As the compound emptied, Poi and Luc noticed one

of the winners of a race limping around the wire at the end of the pier. He then lowered himself on to the ferry and disappeared down a hatch. The guard had long since abandoned his post to join the festivities in the building.

Poi said to Luc, "We are finished. We can't go back or forward. I fear for our loved ones." As he made to go down the hill, Luc said, "No. We have one chance left. As you see, the ferry is left unguarded and the ferryman is lying on the deck. Maybe he is dead. Our only hope is to pull ourselves across the river on the rope and to pull the ferry back over to this side. When we get everybody aboard we cut the rope and let the current take us down the river. But first we must tell the rest, and prepare for darkness."

As darkness closed in, Luc and Poi guided them down the path and along the coast road. They silently walked along towards the pier, aware of other groups hidden well off the road. Those groups were hoping to cross the river on the morning ferry, unaware of the carnage and cruelty that met those who crossed over before. Poi wanted to warn them, but Luc said, "If we manage to pull the ferry across they will all want to go with us, and being so many it would be impossible to hold them back. The danger is that they would take the ferry and we would be left, our last hope gone. If everything will go well for us, there will be no means for them to cross over. So it is best to keep quiet. Once the bandits realise that the ferry has gone, they will make enough noise to alert all to their presence."

When they reached the pier, Luc and Poi told the rest to stay hidden with their packs at the far end of it. They told them that if they were caught on the other side, the rest were to move back to the trees and stay hidden for a day and a night. If they hadn't returned by then, the rest were to make their way along the coast road to the north and ask for help in the first fishing village.

Following the rope down into the water, they pull themselves along it until the rest lose sight of them in the darkness. About half-way across, the rope dips under the water. To keep hold of it, they have to take turn about lifting it to the surface. This soon exhausts them. Luc says, "We will rest for a moment. The worst is over. We are out of the current, and the rope is floating from now on."

With the reflection of the compound lights on the water, Poi can see the rope snaking along the surface to the stern of the ferry. They pull themselves silently along, and reach the ferry. They climb up the framework of the pier until they are level with the ferry's gunnel.

In the dim light coming from the building, they can make out two people on the ferry. One is lying mid-ship below the gunnel. The other, whom they recognise as the ferryman, is sitting with his back propped against the mast crutch. They realise he is watching them.

As they step off the pier timbers on to the ferry, the ferryman lifts his finger to his lips, signalling them to be quiet. Going closer to him they can hear his breath, which is making a faint bubbling sound in his throat. They speak to him. They tell him their plans. They warn him that they are prepared to kill him if he tries to raise the alarm.

He tells them that his name was Shom, and that they are the answer to his prayers. The boat belonged to himself and his brother, but the bandits had taken the brother away two days ago and killed him.

They had run the ferry on the rope every third day and traded up and down the coast in between times. Three days ago, when they went across with a second lot of passengers, the bandits were waiting for them. "I was beaten then," he tells them. And pointing to the person sleeping below the gunnel he says, "And that poor woman was put there."

Luc made to go over to the sleeping woman, who was covered with empty rice sacks and surrounded by baskets. But Shom told him to leave her be, and not to disturb her until they were well clear. He warned them her screams would alert the guards.

Luc began to open the ropes which held the ferry to the pier. Shom told him that he had been going to release the ferry that night, but he was still weak from a beating he had received from a guard during the day. Also he wouldn't have been able to start the engine, because the guard took the ignition keys with him when he left to join the rest. "Now that you and your friends have come to help, we will be able to start it with the handles if you do as I tell you," he says. He guides them, "When you release the rope, we must pull slowly to begin with. This will conserve your strength which you will need when we get to midstream, where the current is stronger."

Pulling silently together, Luc and Poi strained to get the ferry moving. As it gained momentum it required less effort to keep it moving, due to its own weight. The wet rope slid smoothly through the iron rings, fore and aft, guiding the boat across.

When they reached midstream, the flow of the river came against the hull, pushing it downstream and tightened the rope. This slowed the crossing, until Shom grasped the rope and helped pull. By the time they had pulled out of the current, Shom was gasping for breath. He sat on the deck with his back against the bulwark. He told them to stop and fill the water tank with water from the river, through a brass cap in the deck. They were to use a leather bucket. Luc and Poi worked feverishly, taking turns in scooping up endless buckets of water and pouring them into the filter cap in the deck. They worked feverishly, thinking of those on the other side, waiting patiently in the darkness. At last the tank overflowed, and they screwed the cap back on. Pulling on the rope like demons, in spite of their flagging strength, the ferry finally bumped into the pier.

Leaving Poi holding the ferry tight to the pier with a bit of rope for a quick release, if need be, Luc clambered up the steps and vanished silently into the darkness in search of the rest.

About ten minutes passed when Poi, waiting with mounting fear, breathed a sigh of relief when Luc appeared at the top of the steps. Poi could hear the scrapes of shoes and muffled whispers in the darkness, which told him all was well.

As they filed quietly down the steps on to the ferry, piling their bags and packs round the mast, Poi noticed that an extra man had joined them. Going to Luc, he asked who he was. Luc replied that the man had told them about himself. He had been a carpenter in a village to the north, where he had started a small business making stools and tables, living in a hut he had built himself, which was also a workshop. Being of Chinese parents, very few accepted him elsewhere. Finding happiness in the village, he had helped all, and he had made a number of friends and was accepted through time as one of the villagers. Until the men in black came.

One evening a friend came hurrying to the back of his hut so as not to be seen. Speaking to him through an open window, he told him to leave as fast as possible, because the men in black had gathered a number of the villagers and were preparing to kill him and burn his hut. Thanking his friend for the great risk he had taken to his own life to warn him, he gathered his few tools, filled a bag with food and climbed out of the window. Crossing to the edge of the trees he waited hidden while six men gathered round his hut. They quickly barred the doors and windows, sure that he was still inside, then threw oil (which three of them had carried in buckets) over the walls and thatch and set light to it.

Other villagers watched sorrowfully at a distance while the six who set the hut alight laughed and joked.

Turning away he quickly made his way through the forest towards the coast.

Working his way through the trees and undergrowth, keeping away from paths and villages, after five days he reached the coast road and walked south at night, until he arrived at the pier, two or three hours before Luc and Poi.

Staying hidden on the pier, he watched both of them slip into the water and pull themselves along the rope. On the pier, the others, who by now had gathered together beside his hiding place, were peering across the river trying to see what was happening, in the faint glimmer of light from the compound. The silence was broken only by the hushed whispering of the children beside him, who were treating the desperate situation like some kind of a grown up game. He didn't want to frighten them so he pretended to be sick, making retching sounds and whispering for help.

Two of the women and an old man came warily over to his hiding place, asking who he was and how they could help him. Explaining he meant no harm, that his sickness was a sham, knowing they would be less frightened of a sick man than of a man who appeared all of a sudden out of the dark, he told them of his journey and why he had to leave his home, finishing his tale by asking if he could join up with them. Both women agreed, but the old man said the decision would be made by Luc and Poi when they got back with the ferry.

As he picked up his bags and was stepping out of his hiding place, Luc appeared beside him, armed with a short piece of broken bamboo, the sharp jagged end thrust forward.

He had been preparing to stab the stranger who appeared out of the dark until one of the women caught his arm and told him, "This man is a friend. He is one fleeing like ourselves, wishing to join us and to help us." On hearing his story Luc agreed, telling them all to hurry.

Poi released the bit of rope from the pier after making sure his bicycle was secure. Whispering to Luc and the carpenter, he told them to pull on the crossing rope. Pulling quietly along the rope, which felt a lot lighter due to the added strength of the carpenter, they reached midstream where the flow of the river was at its full strength.

Poi went up to the forward ring and told Luc to pull out the pin which was at the bottom of the iron ring holding it in place underneath the gunnel. Before they could release the rings, Shom said, "No. Cut the rope. If we leave the rings on the rope they will just get another boat and continue their carnage, and killing helpless people. It will not be so easy to operate another ferry without the iron rings and I have no wish to return to this place of cruelty ever."

Agreeing, Poi cut through the heavy rope with his knife. The rope parted. The cut ends slipped through the fore and aft rings and dropped into the river.

Free from the rope, the ferry drifted silently down the river with the flow. Those aboard quietly congratulated each other with relief and excitement at escaping the bandits and at last being able to drift down the river.

5

Shom, who by now had recovered enough strength, removed the lashing from the tiller and was steering the ferry, holding her in midstream. After a while he told them that they were far enough downstream to be able to start the engine without the noise alerting those ashore. Asking Luc to take the tiller he told Poi and the carpenter to slide back the hatch cover above the engine and to climb down to the engine. Shouting instructions down to them, on the second attempt the engine made a thudding noise, coughed, picked up speed and then ran smoothly.

By this time Luc, who had never been in a boat before, shouted to Shom that they were going to hit the river bank. Shom grabbed the tiller and swung it hard over. The ferry bounced once or twice in the shallows, before veering back into deep water in the centre of the river.

When Shom asked Luc what happened, he explained that he didn't know how to steer a boat, as he came from a village deep inland and that none of them had ever been in a boat before.

On hearing this, Shom said that he knew of a small island in one of the creeks where they could rest up and hide safely. It was about half a mile from the sea and they could spend the day preparing for the sea voyage along the coast to Cambodia.

Moving down the river with the current, the engine was chugging away at enough revs to give steerage. As the sky was getting brighter they turned into the creek and tied up alongside a small island underneath over-hanging branches that hid them from the main river.

Knowing that they were safely hidden from prying eyes they prepared hot food and, exhausted, they slept soundly. As the sun rose, Luc, who was the lightest sleeper, was woken by a faint moaning. Thinking that it was Shom's breathing, he arose to make sure that he was all right. Treading his way aft, through packs and sleeping people, to where Shom slept, he noticed that the woman who had been lying on the deck, covered with sacks, was now sitting up and rocking slowly back and fore moaning quietly.

Stepping over to her he saw a wire going from the gunnel running underneath the sacks which still covered her. Leaning over her, Luc grasped the sacks and lifted them away from her upper body. He immediately shouted in horror and stepped back. As he did so he stumbled over Poi and his wife, who were sleeping behind him, and he fell four feet down the open hatch of the hold. There he lay, sprawled on top of some bags of rice, shaking with fright. The bags of rice were the remains of the last cargo Shom and his brother were to have delivered further down the coast. By now everyone on the ferry had woken and were gathered round the poor woman, staring and weeping at her agony as if she was some kind of circus side-show.

Shom, the humanitarian, pushed through and told the rest to go back to sleep - that he would attend to her. Cradling her head so as she could drink, he held a bowl of water to her mouth, and she managed to take a few sips.

The poor woman, by a slight twist of fate, had a cleft palate on the right side of her mouth and had been horrendously tortured by the bandits.

A long French bayonet had been thrust from left to right through both her breasts. Where it protruded between her breasts a wire had been wrapped round it and crimped. The other end of the wire had been wrapped around the stringer below the gunnel and nailed, leaving her tethered like an animal. The bandits then put baskets of hashish, some small books, a jar of spirit gum and a ladies small make-up brush beside her.

She had to cut the pages of the books into cigarette papers and fill them with hashish, sticking the edges down with the gum.

Sitting on the deck she was not allowed water until she had filled a basket with cigarettes, having to fill two more before food was thrown at her.

In her agony, tethered by the bayonet through her breasts, she had to roll narcotic cigarettes, which were sold for two or three dollars each, or twelve rounds of ammunition, to the American soldiers. They were flocking daily on to the South, knowing nothing of the pain and agony that had gone into making them, the drug they so eagerly sought - caring even less where it came from.

They bought and bartered for as many as they could get, not realising or caring that the bullets they exchanged for drugs would be used against them in the not too distant future.

Poi's wife, herself heavy with child, pleaded with them to help the woman, telling them that if the bayonet is left in she will die. Agreeing, Poi told the women to hold her down, so as they could unwind the wire from the centre of the bayonet between her breasts. Luc gently unwound the wire and he had just about finished when the woman started to scream with pain and passed mercifully into unconsciousness.

One of the other women supported the breasts, while Poi pulled the bayonet, which came out quite easily, giving thanks that the woman was unconscious. Tearing strips of cloth from one of their packs, they pour spirits from a bottle one of the guards left aboard, over the wounds and bind them with strips of cloth, making her as comfortable as possible.

Luc then said to Shom, "We should be leaving soon, as the longer we stay here the more chance we have of being spotted." Shom, shaking his head, told him, "No. We will wait until dark and sail from island to island, hiding during the day. A number of fishermen have found it profitable to stop and demand what they call 'passage money' from boats travelling along the coast towards Cambodia, using increasing violence, demanding more and more from each boat they stop. First we must make sure that our own boat is undamaged after bumping in the shallows up the river.

"You will have to go below to check there is no water coming in, as my chest pains me, and I fear that I won't be able to climb down into the hold."

Luc clambered down the ladder into the hold, making his way forward under the deck through a small bulkhead door which led to the living accommodation, such as it was. Lifting the floorboards and finding the bilge dry, he made his way to the ladder, coming down into the accommodation from the fore-deck. As he was about to climb the ladder he saw a man lying on one of the bunks watching him with large bulging eyes.

Terrified, Luc leapt up the ladder, through the hatch and ran down the deck to where Shom was sitting. When he told Shom about the man in the fo'c'sle, Shom told him that he already knew.

The man had escaped from the compound and crept aboard with the intention of warning the refugees on the other side of the river when the ferry crossed over again. But as it turned out, having to wait hidden in the ferry, his mind gradually deteriorated, leaving him as you see him now, demented and insane. The bandits in the compound had cut off his and his son's toes, making them run against each other. His son deliberately held back to let his father win and was shot. They then took his wife and made her run against a much younger, lighter woman who finished the race before his wife had covered half the distance. They shot her before she had reached the end of the compound.

He had seemed fine when he crept aboard, but having to wait on his own, hidden in the dark for so long, the atrocities of the compound preyed on his mind until, as you can see now, he is completely insane.

On hearing this, Luc filled a bowl of water and went back down into the fo'c'sle. He tried to make the man drink some of the water by pouring it into his open mouth, but most of it spilled down the side of his face. After he had managed to get him to swallow about a cupful, he picked up a rag which was lying on the bunk and soaking it in the water, washed the man's face and neck to help cool him. Leaving the bowl of water beside him, he went back up the ladder to the others and told them to rest as they would be leaving when the sun went down.

The day passed slowly and the carpenter who was attending to the woman from whom they had removed the bayonet, told them that he had seen this method of punishment before in small villages on the China-Vietnam border. It had been practice on those who they blamed for any minor or major disaster which befell the village. It was always a poor unfortunate person, who from birth had some form of handicap or disfigurement, which they blamed for casting spells and for being witches or wizards.

The methods he saw had always been with sharpened bamboo for the women and a length of bamboo with large thorns tied as hooks at each end for the men they condemned as wizards. Luc told the carpenter that he didn't want to hear any more because of the pressure that he had been under since leaving their homes, and that he was scared that he was going to end up like the poor man in the fo'c'sle.

6

Before darkness fell, Shom told them to make a place for themselves in the hold and instructed the men-folk as to the ropes and other duties that would be required of them to raise the sail, once they were clear of the river and into open water, so as they could make the most of the offshore breeze that blows during the night.

They left the island behind as the sun was going down. Nightfall found them steering a southerly course with the engine stopped and the offshore wind, which always blew well into the early hours of the morning at that time of the year, filling their sail.

Shom told them that he was heading for an island he had used before about twenty miles away. It had a small sheltered bay with a sandy beach where they had beached the ferry a number of times to clean underneath and paint her.

They could see the navigation lights of other boats, some fishing and others steaming on a set course. Telling them to keep a sharp lookout, he explained that a lot of fishermen never bothered to show lights if the fishing was good, so that the others wouldn't know where they were. Also those that had turned to piracy would just sit and wait in the dark for an unsuspecting boat to come along.

Then they would suddenly start their engines, switching on their lights and jump aboard the boat, robbing all. Arriving at the island before dawn, Shom, by now exhausted, had made them lower the sail. He started the engine and motored slowly into the bay, tying the ferry alongside a steep outcrop of rock.

They tied the ferry to the rocks which made a natural pier, making her fast with ropes Shom had left tied ashore the last time he had used the bay. To break the monotony, most of them had gone ashore and were resting on the sand close to the ferry.

Luc and Poi decided to take the children, who were growing restless, for a short walk to the other side of the island. As they reached the other side they saw a boat larger than their own, with about fifty or sixty people aboard, going past in a southerly direction.

Following along the shore so as to keep it in sight, they saw that it was heading in the general direction of two fishing boats which were about two to three miles away. As they watched the boat, which was passing to the east of the fishing boats, they saw them speed up, close in and stop the boat, tying up on either side of her.

Being so far away they couldn't make out what was happening, but could hear the sound of long bursts of machine gun fire. Moving along the coast away from the undergrowth to get a clear view, they waited until they saw the two boats move away at full speed. Then a huge column of water rose out of the sea where the boat with the people had been. Seconds after, the sound of a large explosion reached them making them realise what had happened.

The boat had been stopped and robbed, the people killed so that no tales would be told, then blown up to cover up all proof of its existence.

Returning across the island with the children to the ferry, they told the rest how they had seen the boat blown up and the large number of people murdered.

Shom told them that the tide was flowing from south to north at this time of day, and for all that were able, to search the south end of the island in case anybody had survived and managed to reach the shore.

Spending the rest of the day watching the shore, nothing was found except some small pieces of planking and a bag with a few items of men's clothing with no means of identification.

It was late evening when they returned to the ferry and they asked Shom if it would be safe to leave. He said, "No." They would have to stay another day because the pirates on the fishing boat would be desperate to get ashore to spend their ill-gotten gains. But first they will decide to fish for some time so that they will have a catch to sell at the market and not arouse suspicion on themselves and their deadly trade.

Keeping a watch on the fishing boats from dawn the next day, about midday they saw them start to head off in a westerly direction towards the mainland coast and disappear into the haze coming from the land.

To make sure that the boats didn't return they kept a watch for the rest of that day, returning to the ferry at dusk. Shom by now had gathered enough strength to start preparing to leave. He explained that he was going to sail away from the island to the east then turn south, intending to sail around any pirates that might be lying in wait inshore, before turning west for the Cambodian coast.

First they must make sure that all their belongings are secure and to prepare for a voyage in the open sea as the passage to the island two nights ago was in comparatively sheltered water.

Shom told them, "This way is the only chance we have to escape from the fishing boats which work closer inshore. It will allow us to approach the Cambodian coast in the safety of darkness with dawn breaking as we get closer in. We will find a suitable landing place or river mouth where you will be able to get ashore safely to continue your journey."

Shom had sailed up and down the coast all his life, learning the different currents and winds, exploiting them fully, navigating by stars, wind and sun, as he delivered and uplifted cargoes between Vietnam and Cambodia and all the outlying islands.

They left the island as it was getting dark, on what they thought was the final leg of the journey to Cambodia, which was getting further away as they sailed east away from the coastal shores and the dangers that lay in wait round them.

Sailing east for about two to three hours in a deepening swell, Shom turned the ferry on to a southerly course, telling them to lower the sail as he could tell from the rising sea that a storm was approaching from the north. He told everyone to take shelter in the hold and cover themselves with whatever they could find.

When the storm would hit them, it would be bitterly cold. Luc was to stay with the women and children, while the carpenter and Poi were to stay with him, to help steer and keep the ferry clear of water, taking turns working the bilge pump.

Some hours later, the terrifying strength of the storm hit them - the northerly wind heavy with freezing cold rain, driving them, pushing them south.

Unable to steer a set course because of the strength of the wind and massive waves, they ran south before the storm for two full days, all gradually weakening with the agonising misery of cold and seasickness.

During the afternoon of the second day the wind dropped, leaving a rough confused sea which by nightfall had calmed down to a gentle swell enabling them to prepare food for those able to eat. But the main requirement was for drinks of water and dry clothes.

With the passing of the storm the temperature had risen, leaving steam rising off everything and a clammy airless humidity making it difficult to breathe.

Shom, who stood by the tiller through the full force of the storm, held his boat with its human cargo to the seas, letting them slip under her, with expert knowledge that only a lifetime of experience can bring. Now weakened by his exertions, he said that the storm had driven them too far south to be able to go back to Cambodia.

Their only hope was to carry on to Malaya, which he thought was four days away.

There was enough engine fuel in the tank, for the engine, which he had filled from the barrels in the compound. He told them, "With a favourable wind as we have now we will manage if we are careful with the remaining water left in our water tank."

He then lashed the tiller slightly to port to counteract the push of the sail and the torque of the propeller enabling her to sail on a straight southerly course. Lying down on a pile of empty rice bags beside the tiller, his breath coming in short gasps, he told Luc that his chest pained him and all will be well until daylight as the ferry will sail herself, but to wake him up if the wind changed or increased during the night.

With exhaustion and weakness brought on by seasickness they all slept soundly through the night until Luc was woken by Shom's breathing, which had changed to a deep rasping, and he went to attend to him.

When he went over to him he saw that there was blood coming from his mouth and forming in a pool on the deck below his head.

Shom, who was awake, managed to whisper to him, telling him that he was dying and for them to take down the sail, leaving the rudder as it is and the engine running; they would reach a main shipping route in three days, where they would be picked up and taken to safety.

Wishing them well and saying he was so sorry that he couldn't do any more for them, he also told them to look after the demented man in the accommodation under the fore-deck. Shom died two hours later.

They shifted his body to the fore-deck, where they covered it beside the gunnel with a bit of old sail, deciding not to put it over the side, but to keep it as proof for the authorities in case they would be accused of stealing the ferry. Relieved they were at this decision, because nobody could bring themselves to put the body over the side.

Agreeing that it was the proper thing to do, Poi and the carpenter went down the ladder into the accommodation and between them lifted the poor demented man up the ladder on to the fore-deck, stopping only for bouts of seasickness, which the oven-like heat underneath the deck had increased ten-fold. Weakened by seasickness, they made him as comfortable as possible, bandaging his feet with strips of cloth and giving him water and food, of which he took very little. Leaving him, they attended to the needs of the rest before collapsing with exhaustion for the remainder of the day.

The ferry chugged its way steadily southward on a flat calm sea, underneath a blazing sun. As night fell, the coolness that came with it was a welcome relief, allowing them to move around and clean themselves from sickness and defecation as best they could, and to cook food for those who were able to eat.

After the heat of the day, a cold fog started to rise from the sea, the clinging dampness soaking everything, going from two extremes of unbearable heat during the day to bitter cold at night.

Huddling together in their wet clothes trying to contain as much warmth as possible, they passed the night until the sun rose and burnt away the fog, leaving them drying in the pleasant warmth of the morning, until the cruel heat came again as the sun rose higher.

About mid-morning Poi's wife went into labour and with help from the others, weak as they were, gave birth to a baby daughter, using up most of the remaining fresh water in the process.

Luc and the carpenter, worried about the water situation, agreed to leave the remaining water for the children and Poi's wife. As there were only two days to go before reaching the shipping lanes, they would manage on what they would gather at night from the fog.

When they told Poi about their decision, he agreed, and they spent that night wiping the condensation from all parts of the ferry with cloths, wringing them into bowls and containers, until exhaustion and weakness made them give up.

The ferry chugged on southward for another two days and a night, until the engine started to misfire and stopped altogether, having used up the last remaining drops of fuel in the tank.

They were now motionless on a flat calm sea - without water or food. Both had run out the day before.

7

---

three • dark • days

With only four months' sea time to go before becoming a fully qualified able seaman, having sat my EDH (Efficient Deck Hand) and lifeboat ticket the previous year, I signed on for what I thought was going to be an eleven month MANZ run - Montreal, Australia, New Zealand and then home.

But all that changed.

We left London docks, half-ship, half-loaded, bound for Philadelphia to complete loading for Montreal, where we would discharge and load for Australia and New Zealand. Arriving in Philadelphia thirteen days later our orders had been changed. Our new orders were to discharge our half-cargo in Philadelphia and sail north to Boston to start loading, then south to Wilmington and to complete loading in Savannah.

Leaving Savannah fully loaded to her marks, we set course for Curacao to load bunkers - fuel oil - then through the Panama Canal into the Pacific, bound for Wellington, where we discharged part of our cargo, then steaming through the Cook Straits to Sydney.

We discharged the rest of our cargo in Sydney and steamed light ship, empty, to Brisbane, where we started loading a part-cargo for Hong Kong, completing loading further north in Rockhampton and Townsville.

Leaving Townsville in the early hours of the morning we rounded Cape York and into the Banda Sea, through the navigators' nightmare maze of islands between New Guinea and Borneo.

Steaming on through the Sule Sea, with the Philippines to starboard, we enter the South China Sea and on to Hong Kong where we discharge and load a part-cargo for the UK and a part-cargo for Singapore, which we will discharge there and load a full cargo for Brisbane.

8

I had spent the morning swinging about in a bosun's chair soogeeing down the samson posts on number four hold, preparing them for a coat of paint in the heat of the afternoon. I had finished the last one and was idling round the bottom of it waiting for the bosun to knock us off for smoke-o. Waiting for him to blow his bloody whistle, which we all hated.

He would go, 'pweep'- make fast, 'pweep pweep'- let go, 'pweep pweep pweep'- smoke-o or dinner, 'pweep pweep'- turn to, and so on. He had just about driven the deck crew mad with it all those months.

It was a whistle he said he got from a games mistress in some girls' school in Liverpool on his last leave. He told us that the lanyard was braided from her hair, but it just looked like ordinary horse hair to the rest of us.

Anyway! It was sorted out some weeks later when himself and the chippy were up on the boat deck, plying some sprung planks with hot pitch beside the davits of number two lifeboat. That day somebody was sand and canvassing the taffrails up on the monkey-island, a mind-numbing job. Hearing the bosun blow his whistle, a signal to knock-off for dinner, he decided to stay a few minutes late to fresh-off the rails so as they would be

64

ready-dried with the heat for a coat of varnish after dinner. Washing the rails down with fresh water and drying off the excess with a cloth, he made his way down the ladder to the boat deck.

As he was making his way past number two lifeboat he noticed the bosun's jacket lying on top of the davit winch; beside it a kettle of hot pitch, a ladle and a pair of gloves.

"Oh! the fool," he thought. That 'somebody' put on the gloves, took the whistle out of the jacket pocket, filled the ladle with pitch and poured the hot pitch through the hole on top of the whistle until it overflowed. Putting the ladle and the gloves back in exactly the same position, he blew on the whistle to cool the pitch and scraped the residue from it, leaving it looking untouched. He then placed it back in the jacket pocket, and so as not to be seen, made his way down through the officers' accommodation to the seamen's mess-room for his dinner. There was no mention about his whistle for the rest of the trip, to the relief of the crew.

But I do know that 'somebody' nearly choked himself laughing up on the monkey-island above the bridge, when he saw the bosun take the whistle out of his jacket pocket and tried to blow it for the afternoon smoke-o and it didn't go 'pweep'. He started poking into the hole with the point of his knife and then his marlin spike; when that didn't clear it he held it up to his eyes and tried to peer through the blocked hole. When he realised that someone had got at it, he ripped it from his jacket and threw it as far as he could over the side.

He then stomped to the for'ard end of the boat-deck and roared 'smoke-o' to the boys working on the fore-deck, who immediately collapsed, rolling about, weak with laughter.

Glowering at them for a moment, he did smart about turn and stalked off to his own mess-room. The 'somebody' up on the monkey-island could see his lips moving as he strode past below him, muttering to himself all kinds of curses of what he was going to do if he ever found out who had blocked his whistle. That 'somebody' was ever so thankful that the bosun did not look up.

Anyway, as I was lashing the gantline and the bosun's chair to the ladder-rung of the samson post, I noticed that the engine-beat had changed and that the ship was slowing down. Just as I was thinking the Old Man, the captain, would be snarling down the phone to the engine-room blasting the engineers for another breakdown, the alarm sounded for boat-drill.

As it wasn't normal to slow down for boat-drill, especially now, being only fifteen hours from our ETA in Singapore, our berth would be booked and waiting empty for us, costing money, and that was the main thing the Old Man didn't like, wasting the Company's money.

All my thoughts were then blasted from me when the tannoy burst into life with its usual stuttering and squawking, and the mate's voice whistling and squealing over it, shouting for the motorboat crew only to the boat-deck and standby for launching. The rest of the deck-crew were to connect up the steam-hose on the starboard side, in case we have to repel undesirables. I didn't understand why we needed the steam-hose which we only used to keep the bum-boats away and to stop anybody boarding us while at anchor. Anyway, it wasn't my problem.

I was the bow-man in the motor lifeboat, so I nipped into the accommodation for my lifejacket. Throwing a denim jacket on at the same time, I dashed up to the boat-deck where, by the time I reached, the motor lifeboat had already been swung out by the first and second mate.

As I jumped into the bow, I asked the mate what was happening and he told us that there was a small fishing boat with people aboard drifting off our port bow, and to be careful as there were pirates in these waters who sometimes used fishing boats as a decoy to halt ships.

But this one, as far as he could see through the binoculars, looked in a bad way, full of refugees. Where she came from and what she was doing this far south he couldn't say, unless she had got caught in the blow we had from the north two nights ago.

We were all at our stations and the mate shouted to the bosun to lower away, stopping a few feet above the water so as the second engineer could start the engine. As soon as the Lister started, the bosun shouted and lowered us the few remaining feet into the water.

The sea was flat calm, like a mirror, as we motored round the bow and saw the boat for the first time. She was a typical fishing boat style of about thirty feet with a raked stem and wide counter stern, with most of her beam aft of mid-ships. Her mast had been stepped near mid-ships and I could see the bamboo slats of what we called a junk rig-sail which had been furled and lashed.

As we came closer I could see that the rudder post entered the hull underneath the counter and came through the deck about six feet for'ard of the stern rail where a tiller of about five feet was fixed on top of it.

We circled round her at a distance, watching some people who were lying on the deck, waving at us. Then we moved in and circled round her at about twenty yards.

The mate, still thinking of the pirates' decoy, took a revolver the Old Man had given him out of his pocket. It was a monster of a thing, covered in rust, that looked as if it had started off life in the Boer War. Placing it on the seat beside him, he said, "I hope to fuck I don't have to use this. All I know about these things is that you have to point them and pull something."

By this time, two of the people on the boat had risen up off the deck and were holding their hands out to us, making drinking signs, asking for water.

Realising that they were harmless refugees in a desperate situation, we turned the lifeboat in to go alongside. As the mate put the revolver back into a locker

I heard him saying to the engineer, "Thank fuck for that. I would have probably blown the arse out of our own boat with it." Hearing that didn't do a great deal for my confidence in him to protect us from the so called pirates.

When we bumped alongside, I jumped aboard with the bow rope, and immediately started gagging with the smell of vomit and faeces which was everywhere.

The refugees, being so weak from seasickness and nearly completely dehydrated from dysentery, along with the lack of water, were unable to control their natural body functions and were covered in both where they lay on the deck.

After the initial shock wore off, the mate started throwing tins of water aboard out of the lifeboat stores, which we punctured with our marline spikes and passed round, having to hold the tins for those who were too weak to hold on to them themselves.

I was holding a tin of water for a man with bulging eyes, who had bandages on both his feet. As he gulped the water down, I could see a bicycle lashed to the coaming behind him and I remember thinking, "What on earth is a bicycle doing on a fishing boat in the middle of the South China Sea?"

When all aboard had enough to drink and were feeling a bit more perky, we started taking stock of what was needed and who was aboard.

They were Vietnamese refugees - three children between six and nine years old, three youngish men and an old man, three women of which one seemed to be sick and a small baby; making eleven people in all.

We then hauled the first-aid chest out of the lifeboat and broke the seal on it, giving all who could take them two seasick tablets each. We had to crush the tablets with the flat blades of our knives and mix them with a little water for two of the women and the man with the bulging eyes, as they were too weak to swallow them whole. It was amazing how well the three youngish men responded to the seasick tablets and water. Within no time, they were smiling and nodding, trying to communicate with odd words of English in a Vietnamese accent which completely baffled us.

I think that they were thanking us, and embarrassed at the mess they were in. When one of them came to me and made washing signs with his hands, I took two steel buckets and a deck brush out of the lifeboat and gave them to him. He gave one of the men the other bucket, which they immediately filled with sea-water and started washing themselves and the deck. Watching them, a terrible feeling of hopelessness came over me, seeing these people in such a helpless state.

I knew that I couldn't leave them, abandoning them to fend for themselves on a sea of which they knew so little of its ways, if anything at all.

The agonies they must have suffered, then to get their hopes dashed as they would watch us sail away, abandoning them once again.

It was then that I decided that I just could not leave them to go back to my 'trouble-free steel world'.

A blast from the ship's siren shattered the air and the mate started signalling back to the ship in Morse Code with one of the lifeboat torches. Receiving a reply with an Aldis lamp from the bridge, he told us all to go back into the lifeboat as we were going to return to the ship for more water and food for the refugees, so that they would have enough supplies to reach land.

By this time, the engineer had been down below having a look at the engine. He said that it was reasonably new and in excellent condition. All that is needed was fuel and a top-up with oil in the reduction gear-box. When the rest of the crew took up their stations in the motor lifeboat, and as the engineer started the engine, the mate called out to me to hurry up. I looked round at the pleading faces I was going to leave behind, and told him that I was not going back on board. "We are only fifteen hours out of Singapore. All we need is diesel fuel, food and water. We can't leave these people here. They don't know anything about boats or the sea and if they did they are in no condition to be able to help themselves."

He went very quiet for a few moments. Looking from stem to stern of the fishing boat and at the refugees, he shook his head and said, "I will tell the Old Man and it will be for him to decide."

As they were about to pull away, the engineer told them to wait so he could make a list of what was needed for the engine. He then jumped back aboard and disappeared down the hatch to the engine. When he came back up the hatch he told the mate to bring three forty-five gallon drums of diesel fuel, three gallons of engine oil and a gallon of gear oil and that he would stay aboard to check the engine until they came back with the stores.

As the motor lifeboat made her way back to the ship, the engineer went down to the engine and I was left on deck, amongst eleven silent people, wondering what I had let myself in for.

My first thought was to check the hold and bilge for water, so I jumped down into the hold amongst the women and children. I landed on top of bags full of rotten mushy rice, which burst with my weight, giving off such an overpowering smell that I nearly passed out.

Keeping low to the floorboards where the smell wasn't so bad, I lifted a small hatch in the boards and checked for water. Finding nothing to worry about, I replaced the hatch and scrambled back up to the deck and fresh air, away from that putrid smell, wondering how on earth the people down there could stand it.

As I was sitting on the hatch-coaming, trying to get my breath back, the engineer came up from below and started working on some wires beside me on the coaming. He told me that there was an electric start on the engine, but no key. So he had fixed it in a way that when I wanted to start the engine, all I had to do was to touch the two wires on the coaming together. The gear-lever for ahead and astern came through a slot in the deck beside the tiller, which I could see was lashed slightly to port. Beside it was an iron rod with a wooden ball on top of it, which he said was the throttle - pull it up for fast, push it down for slow.

As he was instructing me on operating the engine, saying that I wouldn't have any problems once we got fuel, the lifeboat alongside the ship started up. As it headed back over to us, I could see that it was a lot lower in the water with the weight of supplies and fuel. Also, I could see the twin towers of the bosun and the chippy, both of whom were over six foot and just as wide. I was sure the Old Man had sent them over to physically remove me back to the ship, which made me more determined than ever to stay.

As I was preparing myself for a one-sided battle, picturing myself being tied and hauled back aboard the ship with a gantline, the lifeboat came alongside and the bosun leapt across, landing on the deck beside me like a huge cat. Thinking that it would be a lot less painful for me if I could knock myself out, I started what I knew was going to be my one and only swing at him.

It connected on the side of his head and sent him sprawling across the gunnel. Before I could get another swipe at him, he held up his hand and growled, "Pack it in you daft bastard. The Old Man sent us across to check and make sure that this fucking rice bowl will stay afloat until you get to Singapore."

Completely taken aback and deflated after being so hyped up, all I wanted to do was to sit down and get my thoughts together.

The first thing was to get rid of the smell and when I told the bosun, who was still speaking to me as if nothing had happened, he said that the poor buggers have been eating the rotting rice which is the main cause of their dysentery. He shouted to the mate to give everyone aboard a dose of kaolin out of the first-aid chest to dry them up.

He then organised the crew into a chain and started dumping the rice over the side, telling them that it had started fermenting and the fumes of it in the confined space was mostly the cause of sickness in the women and children down in the hold. When some of the bags hit the water, the rotten sacks burst and the rice seemed to swim off in all directions, doing all kinds of manoeuvres with the amount of maggots in it. I remember thinking that they must have been starving to eat it and no wonder they were sick.

While all this was happening, the chippy had been examining the boat and was now back in the lifeboat, which he had moved round the stern so as he could inspect the rudder pintles and gudgeons underneath the wide counter.

When he finished inspecting the boat he told the mate that she was in excellent condition and that she had never been used for fishing. She was typical of the type that can be seen all round the Vietnamese coast, fetching and carrying all types of cargo. But that this one had at some time been used as a ferry.

When the mate asked how he could tell, he pointed to the iron rings fore and aft in the gunnel and said it was a system that they used on rivers so that they would not have to manoeuvre too much on the narrow, confined channels. Usually when they finished ferrying, they left the iron rings on the rope so that it would be easier to connect up again, but somebody must have cut the rope to release this one!

By now all the stores had been transferred and the engineer was siphoning diesel from a drum into the fuel tank, which was an old lorry fuel tank sitting on the deck in a wooden frame, with a pipe going down into the engine. He showed me how to siphon, first putting a long hose halfway into the drum and the other end into the tank. Then a shorter length of about nine inches is placed in the top of the drum and a cloth jammed into the hole to seal round both pipes so as not to allow any air to escape. You then blow into the short length of pipe, and the air forces the fuel along the longer pipe into the fuel tank. This system works well and prevents you getting a mouthful of fuel, but you must remember to push the pipe further down as the drum empties.

He then touched the two wires on the coaming together and the engine churned round for a moment or two and chugged into life running smoothly as if it had never stopped.

The captain must have seen the puff of smoke from the exhaust when the engine started, and impatient to get going again sounded the siren three times as a signal for the lifeboat to return if all was well.

After ordering everybody back into the lifeboat, the mate said to me, "The decision for you to stay is up to yourself. But the captain said that he will have to mark you down as absent without leave, and will probably have to log you a week's pay." I told him I that I was going to stay anyway so it didn't matter, and for him to do as he must.

One of the refugees, whose name I would find out later, opened a pack and took out a flat parcel which he offered to the engineer, repeating in broken English, "You stay, you stay," and pointing at the deck. Opening the parcel, the engineer unfolded a woman's silk dress with a red and scarlet design woven through with gold thread. He shook his head and pointed to me saying, "He stay, he stay." Then, rolling the dress up, he handed it back to him.

By now the bosun was growling at everybody, trying to get them back aboard the lifeboat and away. As he stepped across into the lifeboat, he said, "There's no compass aboard." He handed me the compass out of the lifeboat, at the same time shaking my hand, wishing me good luck and saying, "I still think that you're a daft bastard, and I will be wanting that compass back in Singapore."

Shaking my hand, the mate told me that I was nuts, and to steer south by west on the compass and that course would make up for any leeway, also not to worry about the weather as there is a high pressure covering the whole area as far south as Sumatra and Java.

Shouting to the engineer to come back aboard, he took up his position at the lifeboat's tiller. When the engineer jumped in and started the engine, he shouted to me that the boat's engine would be fine but to remember to keep topping up the fuel tank from the drums.

As they started to move away the refugee moved to the side of the fishing boat and threw the parcel containing the dress to him shouting, "You keep, you keep. Thankyee, thankyee." Before they left the ship, I had started taking stock of the water and stores. Looking at it all I thought there was enough there to last fifty people three months. The water was in eight five gallon containers which I recognised as the drums used for the bread oil that the bakers used in the galley. How there were eight of them empty I couldn't figure out, because each one as it was emptied was claimed by the lampy and taken aft to his locker in the poop-deck. A prized possession for mixing his paint in, after he cut the top off it.

I found out to my cost later that the crew had poured the oil into the only reasonably clean container on the ship, the captain's bath, the only bath on the ship, and had blasted the containers out with the steam hose before filling them with fresh water.

Stowing everything as best I could, I came across two metal containers and wondering what was in them I opened one and thought, "The chief steward, bless him, ever thoughtful!" He had emptied out two aluminium Wall's ice cream containers, with the clip-on sealed tops, and stuffed them full of toilet rolls and paper towels, with a note on top wishing me luck, and that I owed him a beer when I reached Singapore.

Busily stowing everything, I hadn't taken much notice of the people aboard, or the ship across from us, until I heard her engines starting up and she started moving off, sounding six blasts on her siren.

As she steamed past me I could see the officers waving to me from the bridge and boat deck. The deck crew of which I had been part were all gathered aft, waving and shouting, making drinking signs with their hands and pointing south to Singapore.

As the ship got further away, a terrible feeling of emptiness and hopelessness came over me, causing me to lose all reason and sense, making me panic and believe that I could catch up with my fast-disappearing ship, which had been my home, with all my friends on board, for the past year.

Panicking, I slammed the gear-leaver forward with my foot and pulled the throttle lever up as far as it would go.

Grabbing the tiller, I tried swinging it to starboard, taking the boat round on course to follow the ship, but it wouldn't move. In my panic I had forgotten that it had been lashed. Desperately I slashed the lashing with my knife and took her round so as her stem was pointing at the stern of my ship, which had slowed down ahead of me.

Thinking that the Old Man had changed his mind and that he was wanting me back aboard, my spirits soared and the feeling of emptiness lifted from me. Because I knew that once I came alongside I would be up the pilot ladder like a monkey back on board, forgetting all about the poor refugees and my great intentions and sympathy for them.

But it wasn't to be; they were watching me on the radar, wondering why I was taking so long to get under way. Thinking that I had problems they slowed down until they saw that I was steaming, heading on a course towards them, everything fine. They then gave two blasts on the siren and moved off towards the horizon, leaving me.

9

t h r e e • d a r k • d a y s

I carried on for about an hour, following in the disturbed calm wake left by the ship, which had long since disappeared over the horizon.

By now I had calmed down, and started to think rationally again. First to take stock of my situation and work out some sort of watch-keeping system and to show a bit more compassion to the refugees, who I had been more than willing to abandon less than an hour ago, who had sat and lain on the deck, silently watching my panicking efforts and blundering, no doubt wondering with apprehension what this fool who had come aboard was going to do next.

I looked at the sea slowly passing alongside us and realised that we were only doing about four knots, if that. Which in anybody's mind meant that fifteen hours in a ship doing twelve knots would cover a greater distance than a fishing boat doing maybe four knots for fifteen hours. The passage to Singapore was going to take a lot longer than I first thought.

Thinking to myself that this is ridiculous, I will have to stop to organise the refugees into watches, find out their names, make food and prepare for steaming through the night. Shutting down the throttle, I pulled the gear-lever back to the centre of the slot in the deck leaving us cruising to a halt. I then lashed the lifeboat compass to the mast-crutch, where I would be able to see it whilst standing at the tiller. When I checked the compass I found out that it hadn't been filled with paraffin, leaving it useless at night, without a light.

Trying to speak to the refugees, I found out that the three fit men's names were Luc, Poi, and the other one I called Carp, because he had been a carpenter. The women's and children's names I was told but couldn't pronounce. I started to show them how to steer the boat, which was an impossible task as none of them had been on a boat before. They just could not understand that when you push the tiller one way the boat will turn the opposite way.

We got her scrubbed down and started preparing food; first more seasick tablets all round, mixing them with a little water as before for the man with the bulging eyes, and whose name no-one knew.

I opened a five pound tin of corned beef, which was more like soup with the heat and poured it into a bucket. Then, breaking up one of our dozen loaves into it, I emptied a tin of Nestles condensed milk, of which we had two cases, in amongst it and mixed up the lot into a smooth paste.

Luc went round everybody forcing them to eat and feeding those who weren't able to feed themselves, making sure that everybody ate something.

As Luc was going round feeding the rest, I had punctured two holes in three tins of condensed milk and gave one each to the children. I could tell that they had never tasted it before, by the look of surprise and sheer enjoyment on their faces as they sucked the thick sweet milk through the holes in the tin.

Poi and Carp were cutting slices from a ten pound round of cheese and passing them round with a mixture of orange juice, water and breakfast rolls, of which we had two sackfuls.

By now everyone had come up on deck out of the hold except one woman who seemed to be ill, and an old man who kept fiddling with a length of stick. The man with the bulging eyes never moved or uttered a word as the rest were eating, but swallowed some of the corned beef paste which I had thinned down with water so as it was more of a drink.

When everyone was fed and seemed a bit more happy I got under way again. The heat was a killer. It just sapped your strength and already one of the five gallon drums of water was empty. But as the day wore on, a breeze of about force two to three started up from the east, blowing steady, helping to cool us and making life a bit more bearable.

I had given up trying to teach them how to steer, and resigned myself to the tiller, sitting on the empty water container my eyes glued to the compass, the card steady on south by west. After a while I found that all I had to do to hold her on course was to keep the tiller slightly to port allowing her to more or less self-steer.

So I spliced the lashing that I had cut in my panic earlier in the day, and looped it over the tiller. Watching the compass, the boat veered maybe two degrees either side of her course in the slight swell, always coming back to settle on south by west. Quite pleased with myself, I started to roll a cigarette. As I lit it I saw the rest watching me and an awful feeling of remorse came over me, when I thought of how eager I had been to get back aboard my ship, leaving them helpless and lost, unable to fend for themselves.

Putting those thoughts behind me I called Luc, Poi and the one I called Carp over to me and started trying to have a conversation with them. Luc and Poi had a smattering of English between them, but all that Carp could do was draw with the charcoal sticks they used for cooking.

As they kept nodding and saying, "Thankee, thankee," after everything I said, I told them to watch the compass and to tell me when the south by west mark which I showed them moved from the line, because I was going to go into the hold to check the bilge for water. Before I jumped down into the hold, I looked back at them, and they looked so tensed watching the compass that they reminded me of three dogs at a rabbit hole expecting the rabbit to pop out anytime.

When I jumped down into the hold, the fearful heat

hit me. It was terrible; airless and smelly, with the added smell and heat from the engine which was on the other side of the bulkhead. Wanting out of there at once, I quickly checked the bilges, which were empty. On my way back up, I noticed that the woman who was lying on the boards seemed to be panting and moaning quietly.

Climbing back out of the hold, I called the three round the compass to come and lift the woman out of the hold up on to the deck, where at least she wouldn't have to suffer the added heat and smell of the engine. As they were lifting her up, I gave the compass a quick check and noticed that the breeze had died down and the card steady on south by west, steering a dead-straight course. By now they had taken the woman up, and placed her in a sitting position with her back supported against the gunnel.

There was still sickness on the side of her face and chin, so I soaked up some paper towels in water and tried to clean her. As I wiped round her mouth I thought that she had been badly beaten, until I realised that she had a slight hare-lip on the right side of her mouth. When reached across to soak the towel again, I must have brushed against the sacks that were covering her, causing them to fall off her shoulders, because, as I started wiping the vomit off her chin, some water ran from the wet towels and landed under the edge of the sacks soaking one of her breasts. She started screaming and writhing in agony, loosening off the sacks, which fell around her waist.

At the time, I could not fully understand what I was seeing. Both her breasts were swollen badly up to her shoulders and underneath her arms, with weeping punctures on both sides, which were an angry mottled scarlet that I recognised from my lifeboat first-aid as infection.

When the sacks slipped down and she started screaming, I froze in shock and horror at what I was seeing, and the agony of the poor woman. I kept repeating in both English and Gaelic, "I'm sorry, I'm sorry. I only wanted to help! I didn't mean to hurt you." As I was repeating this over and over again in my stunned trance, I could feel someone pulling at my arm, harder and harder each time, until he made me turn round. Luc was pulling me by the arm towards the lifeboat's first-aid chest, pointing to it saying, "You fix, you fix, you fix lady."

At first in my dazed state I thought something had broken in the boat, and that we were sinking. Until he took me to the chest and opened the lid, pushing my hand inside it amongst the bandages and continually repeating, "You fix, you fix lady."

That was when I came to my senses, with my hand being held in the first-aid chest and a Vietnamese man's face inches away from my own, shouting at me, "You fix, you fix, you fix lady."

At last I realised what was needed. I searched the chest for pain-killers. Finding the tin, I crushed two omnopon with my knife and put them in a bowl with half a cup of water, which I gave to her while Luc held her head steady.

It took about three or four minutes before her breathing began to settle to what I thought was a reasonable sign that the omnopon was easing the pain. As I was checking her pulse, holding her right hand in my left hand and feeling her wrist with my right hand, I felt what I thought was her hand tighten on my hand with a spasm of pain. When I looked up at her, she opened her eyes and looked at me, gripped my hand and smiled painfully at me, thanking me the only way she could in her painful condition.

The moment I felt her hand tighten on me, thanking me, a weight seemed to lift from my mind and body.

Somehow I knew that everything was going to be all right, as if something or somebody was watching over us, guiding us. We lifted up the old bandages that had slipped down round her waist, and covered her with the sacks leaving her to sleep, breathing normally.

All the time I was tending to the woman, I noticed that the other women treated her with a kind of cool indifference and seemed to keep their distance from her.

When I asked Luc and Poi in sign language and broken English what the problem was, I understood that because of her disfigurement they thought that she was some sort of shaman or witch, and were scared that she would cast a spell on them. On hearing this, I went into a terrible temper. The thought of letting the injured woman suffer so much because of some stupid superstition made my blood boil.

When I looked, they had gone back into the hold and were sitting there contentedly, drinking water and eating breakfast with not a care in the world.

I snatched a short broken length of bamboo with a jagged end on it from the deck and jumped down into the hold, waving it at them, shouting and pointing at the injured woman threatening to hit them with it unless they attended to her.

I sure made myself understood. They scrambled out of the hold with a flurry of bread rolls, water and lampshade hats and started to bathe her with fresh water, fussing round her making her comfortable.

Expecting Luc and Poi to give me trouble for chasing their womenfolk, I turned round quickly, ready with the bamboo, and to my amazement they were laughing and clapping, nodding to me shouting, "Yess, yess. Good, good."

I couldn't believe it. They were enjoying my escapade in the hold as if it was some kind of pantomime. I thought again, "Strange people."

I dropped the bamboo in the hold and took fresh bandages and sulpha powder, at least I think it was called

10

As night was drawing in, the little wind that was left died away altogether, leaving us chugging along at four knots on a flat calm sea. I was worried at not having any oil for the compass light, so I filled it with diesel fuel which totally blackened the lens with soot as soon as I lit it.

The night passed slowly for me, with the tiller lashed, checking the compass every half hour or so with my Ronson lighter, which served me well for a number of years afterwards, until the salt water and damp worked their way underneath the leather cover and corroded through the small gas tank. On occasions when I checked the compass, I had to make slight adjustments to the tiller, but most times she was steering dead true.

During the night Poi, Luc and Carp took turns keeping me company. I could hold a conversation with Poi and Luc, but couldn't make heads nor tails of anything Carp was trying to say, so the others gave me the gist of his journey, which hadn't been an easy one.

The night passed uneventful until daybreak, when the injured woman started to whimper and moan with pain, the effects of the pain-killers wearing off, so I gave her two more omnopon tablets, which she took with sips of water and settled down to sleep peacefully within five minutes.

She seemed to be a lot stronger and breathing close to normal, which I put down to proper food and water.

When I went back to the tiller, I asked Luc and Poi what had happened to her and why she had been shot, because the wound looked to me as if a bullet had passed straight through her. I held my arms up as if I was holding a rifle and said bang! Immediately both of them shook their heads and held up their arms making thrusting movements, repeating, "Bayonet, bayonet."

As I listened with mounting horror, they told me what had happened to her and the cruelty that had been inflicted on her by those mindless subnormal people, if people is the right word for them.

As they explained, Poi was drawing diagrams on the deck with charcoal and Luc was pointing to a number of small baskets which were covered with bits of tarpaulin and to a wire that I hadn't noticed before, lying underneath the gunnel. When they finished telling me, there was nothing I could say. I didn't want to believe that people could do such things to others.

But it was all there before me, and Luc and Poi must have sensed the horror and aggression for those people that was building up inside me. Because as I rose from my seat at the tiller, they both moved quickly to the other side of the boat, watching me as I passed the sleeping woman and pulled the wire from underneath the gunnel, giving it one heave, snapping it where it was nailed to the stringer and throwing it over the side.

I then went to the baskets and lifted the bits of tarpaulin off them. Two of them were full of cigarettes and one was half full. The rest were full of shredded tobacco, books, two jars with some kind of paste in them, a small brush and scissors. I looked at the sleeping woman for a moment or two, thinking how she must have suffered.

Then in a frenzy I started throwing the baskets and everything else I could find, that had to do with her agony and suffering, over the side. When the last basket was going over, I heard Luc shouting at me. When I had calmed down enough to look at him, I saw that he was making money signs with his forefinger and thumb. I wasn't sure at first what he was on about until he explained slowly to me, and then I knew.

Luc, always the businessman, even in the middle of an ocean, had covered the baskets to keep them dry, planning to sell the cigarettes when, if ever, they reached land. When I asked him why he would do such a thing, his answer was, "The cigarettes were there, why waste them, because there is a big demand for them and they would have made a lot of money to give to the woman who was so cruelly forced to make them." I couldn't answer him, so I went aft to sit quietly by the tiller my mind in a complete turmoil.

Luc and Poi went down into the hold amongst the women and their children, and within two minutes of them joining them I started to hear high pitched shouting in their own language.

Luc and Poi jumped up out of the hold and came to join me at the tiller. The women then came out of the hold and started to attend to the injured woman, bathing her and dressing her in clothes that they took from their own packs. As they started feeding her, Poi turned to me smiling and nodding said, "No more problem, they fix, they fix."

When they went down into the hold they must have read the riot act to their women-folk because when they asked me for sulpha powder to put on the wounds with clean bandages, she had been dressed in the best of clothes. She had also been fed, and other clothes from the packs had been spread around her as a mattress and support against the slight motion of the boat.

As the morning passed, the sun burnt away the mist and fog, leaving the day hot and airless. At about two hours later, the same breeze as yesterday started, blowing force two to three, steady from the east.

I was at the tiller looking over the side, thinking that at this speed we would take a week to reach Singapore. I suddenly remembered what my father used to say to me when we would be out fishing with our own boat at home. I would have the engine running and he would say to me in Gaelic, our native tongue, "Nach cuir thu dheth an donas fuaim agus fàileadh tha sin agus cuir an-àird an seòl mar bu chòir." (Will you turn off that devilish noise and smell and put up the sail as you should).

Of course the sail! If I put it up in this breeze we might

be able to get another knot or two out of her if we were lucky.

I left the tiller and went up to the mast to try and figure out the rigging. This was the first time that I had been close to a junk-rig and wasn't very sure how to set it, but it looked straight-forward enough.

The man with the bulging eyes beside the mast hadn't moved. Carp fed him and gave him water, which he took when it was put to his mouth. All the time he stared straight ahead, never uttering a word.

All the time that I had been examining the mast and rigging, I was getting a horrible, sour kind of smell. As I followed the mast stay with my eyes from the top of the mast down to where it was shackled to a bottle screw fixed in the gunnel, I noticed what I took to be a bundle of old sail tucked tight against the timberheads.

Moving closer to it, the smell became stronger. So, thinking that the sail was covering more rotten rice, I dragged it clear with the intention of throwing it overboard. Until I saw what the cover had been concealing.

Once I had dragged the sail clear, I saw the body of a Vietnamese man, wearing an old pair of faded, green shorts, lying on the deck.

When I was dragging the sail it must have been tucked underneath him, causing the body to turn over on to his back, enabling me to see the imprint of the timberheads at regular spacings from his shoulder to his ankle. This had been caused by the body being placed hard up against the timbers. I could also see an indentation on the right side of his chest, the size of a large pudding plate. I remember thinking that for a hollow like that to be in someone's chest, all his ribs must have been broken and the ends must have damaged something inside him, causing his death at the time or shortly afterwards.

Gathering up the cover, I threw it back over him and staggered in a daze aft to the tiller. I wondered when the nightmare was going to end and what other grisly finds would be waiting for me, especially underneath the fore-deck, as I hadn't had time to have a look in there yet.

Sitting at the tiller, feeling as drained as the empty water container I was sitting on, I looked at Luc, Poi and Carp who were sitting very quiet on the coaming, their heads bowed, staring at the deck.

I thought for one fearful moment that they had killed him and that I would be next, until I reasoned with myself, that if they had killed him, why didn't they throw the body that had obviously been dead for some time overboard.

The more I thought about it the more I realised that those aboard were not capable of killing anyone, and that it just wasn't in their nature.

The silence was broken by Carp who came over to me with a bowl of water, muttering something in his own language which sounded to me as if he was praying.

When Luc and Poi joined us, they all started to

explain together, with Carp doing his charcoal drawings on the deck. By the time they had finished telling me, I was filled with so much sadness for Shom, the owner of the boat, whose body lay on the fore-deck covered by a bit of old sail, that all I wanted to do was cry and hug Luc and Poi, offering some kind of comfort for the suffering and hardships they had endured.

Once I had got over my find on the fore-deck, we filled the fuel tank and made food for everyone. Corned beef, soup and bread, followed by tins of sliced cling peaches, followed by tins of condensed milk which was sucked out of the tins through one of the two holes made in the top with my spike.

I also gave another two omnopon tablets to the women to give to the injured woman, who seemed to be a lot stronger. The omnopon and sulpha powder were working.

But as I was sitting on my container, the smell of the body on the fore-deck was getting stronger, and catching in my throat.

Knowing that I would have to do something about it, that there was no point in putting off the inevitable, I rose and walked slowly up the deck to the body. I picked it up and dropped it over the side, with the old sail still wrapped round it. Keeping my eyes on the deck, I walked past the rest back to the tiller, and had to physically stop myself from looking astern for the next half hour.

After I had put the body over the side, I was sitting at

the tiller for about ten minutes, when everyone, who by now had gathered in the hold, started muttering and lighting splints of wood which gave off a sweet smell as they burned. I think they were saying prayers for Shom, that courageous and compassionate man whose body I put over the side with as much reverence as I would have an empty cardboard box.

I felt in my mind that I had committed an awful crime and tried to justify it by convincing myself that I had done it to prevent any sickness or disease spreading to the people aboard the boat, who were weak enough as it was.

When I had calmed down I tried to roll a cigarette, which I managed to do on my third attempt because my hands were shaking so much.

As I was smoking it, I saw the woman whom I knew as Poi's wife sitting on the coaming. She had mixed some condensed milk with water in a bowl and was taking a sip from the bowl and putting the milk into the baby's mouth from her own mouth, drop by drop.

It was heart-wrenching to watch that sorely distressed mother, desperately trying to keep her new baby alive, for another day, even another hour, with so little.

As we chugged on I had lost all interest in trying to put the sail up. I just kept thinking and saying to myself, "What next? What the hell will happen next?"

But I was determined more than ever to get these people safely ashore, and to finish the journey Shom had started and given his all for. I felt that I couldn't let him down. Even though I had never spoken to him I felt that I had known him and that his presence was still with us.

During the evening the wind dropped and we were again crossing a flat, glassy sea, which all of a sudden seemed to boil white about a mile away to the east of us. It seemed to boil and bubble in a patch about two miles long in a north and south line and as far as the horizon to the east. I have no idea as to the cause of the disturbance, but it was quite frightening at the time.

As we steamed through the night, Poi and Luc continued to keep me company at the tiller. I could read the compass by the light of the moon, which seemed so big and close that I felt I could hit it with a stone. It was so bright that I could see the horizon all round, and even the smallest detail aboard the boat.

Luc and Poi told me about the murders they saw being committed at the bridge on the river and the death of their own mother. This seemed to depress me even more than I had been during the day. So I told them to be quiet as I wanted to sleep for a while, and for them to watch the compass, making sure they woke me up if the card turned more than two of the black lines away from the big black line. I then stretched out on the deck underneath the tiller and slept like a log.

It was daylight when I woke up, and Luc and Poi were still staring at the compass card as if they were waiting for it to explode. As I started to get up off the deck, I got tangled in clothes that Luc and Poi had covered me with during the night. They had also rolled up other items of clothing and placed them under my head as a pillow. I must have been completely exhausted before they could do that without waking or disturbing me. I remember thinking that I would have given anything for a cup of tea or coffee, but I had to make do with a tin of orange juice.

They told me that they had seen a number of lights during the night, away in the distance, which made me very worried. We were steaming along without any navigation lights, getting closer by the hour to one of the world's busiest sea routes. My first thought was to go down the hatch to check the engine, before the heat of the day made it unbearable in the small engine room. The engine had been chugging along hour after hour without any problem, apart from when it seemed to lose power and belched out thick black sooty smoke for thirty anxious seconds yesterday, which I put down to clearing itself out.

I checked that everyone was still in good health and fed, but there was no need to. They were now looking after themselves, with the two women looking after the injured woman, and Carp tending to the man on the fore-deck, with the bulging eyes.

I then went down the hatch to the engine and stopped it to check the oil which needed topping up. I put about half a gallon of fresh oil into the sump and was checking all the pipes and connections as I worked my way back to the hatch, when I heard water trickling in somewhere under the boards round the stern. As the level in the bilge looked pretty much the same I knew that it wasn't too bad a leak, but I though I would check it out anyway. And was I glad I did! The two nuts had worked loose on the stern tube packing gland, which seals the hull where the propeller shaft goes through the stern post.

The gland had come away from the packing and as I watched, what had been a trickle of water was gradually developing into a fast-flowing major leak, which would soon fill the boat. I pushed the gland back into the packing, tightening the nuts with a shifting spanner that I found in the tool box, which was beside a box that held two twelve volt batteries needed to start the engine.

Giving thanks to everything that I could think of to give thanks to for spotting the leak in time, I went back up on deck and touched the two wires on the coaming together. The engine started immediately.

When we were underway again I went back down to the engine for a final check on the stern tube, which was dry. In the passing I gave two turns to a leaver on top of a big grease container which pushed the grease along a pipe to the stern tube greasing the shaft.

As I was making my way back to the ladder below the hatch, I noticed some electrical wires running along the deck-head, passing through the aft bulkhead to the hold. With the lights of ships seen during the night still on my mind, the wires made me think that there must be some kind of lighting system aboard. So I followed the wires back to where they went into a junction box, connecting to a switch above the battery box. That was it! I went back up, checked the course, and then jumped down into the hold, landing between the woman and children, who all scattered out of my way, no doubt thinking that I was going to chase them out up on to the deck again. I made signs that it was all right for them to stay.

They stayed in the hold with me, but moved in a bundle from one part of the hold to the other, keeping the same distance from me all the time, as I followed the wire through a small door into the accommodation below the fore-deck, if you could call it accommodation.

It was a space with four bunks, a small table fixed to the bulkhead and a charcoal stove with a hopper over it to catch the smoke and fumes, diverting them up a pipe to a hole in the deck. The heat in there was fearful, so it must have been unbearable with the stove lit when they would be cooking their food. The wire stopped at a bank of four switches on the bulkhead inside the door.

From one switch, I followed two wires to a plug which was in a small box in the hold above the door. By now the heat had started to affect me, so I went back up to the tiller, to the relief of those in the hold.

Explaining to Luc and Poi what I was looking for, they disappeared into the accommodation and reappeared about fifteen minutes later, smiling and nodding, holding what looked to me like a handful of eels. Thick heavy duty cable, the cable for the navigation lights. Luc took the cable up on deck and began to untangle it, while I showed Poi where to place the lights, which were on two short lengths of bamboo, into the holes in the gunnel, port and starboard.

There were only two lights, red and green, which were fixed in such a way that they could easily be removed when the boat was attached to the rope, being used as a ferry.

Round about midday, the wind started blowing steady about force three to four from the east. I loosened off the lashing from the sail and thought, "Here goes. In for a penny in for a pound." As we hauled on the downhaul, the sail seemed to leap up on its own, opening like a giant fan and swinging round the mast, making the boat heel slightly to starboard and surge forward as it filled.

It was unbelievable. We didn't have to tension or trim the sail, it all seemed to be automatic. A far superior sail to the lugsails we used at home. The bamboo slats seemed to be adjusting the sails, to get the maximum power from the wind.

On we went, the engine pushing and the sail pulling. To my mind, this boat had been built for sailing, the sail just steadied her in the slight swell, leaving her with a very easy soft motion, which made life for those suffering from seasickness a lot more comfortable.

The wind being deflected down from the sail on to the deck also helped to cool the injured woman on the deck, and those in the hold. I had to adjust the tiller slightly, lashing it a wee bit more to port to hold her self-steering on south by west.

As I was sitting on my container, quite pleased with myself at managing to get the sail up with so little effort, increasing our speed to about four or five knots and steadying the boat so much, I noticed a rope tail coming out from behind the stringer below the gunnel. As I went up the deck to tidy it away, the old man in the hold reached out over the coaming and touched the back of my leg with a stick.

Since I had come aboard the boat, every time I passed him he tried to (what I thought) trip me up. So as I was going back and fore, up and down the deck, I would have to swerve round him to avoid him every time he leaned out of the hold with his bloody stick.

This time I thought, "That's it, I'm not putting up with this any more." I snatched the stick out of his hand and was about to throw it over the side, when the women in the hold started shouting at me in their own language. Luc and Poi were shouting at me in broken English, "You stop, you stop." Carp was shouting at me in a completely different language, and the three children started to cry.

As I was standing there with the stick in my hand, wondering what the devil was going on, Poi took the stick from me and gave it back to the old man. The look of horror on his face disappeared, and was replaced with smiles and nods.

As Poi rattled off a speech to him, that I couldn't understand, I knew that I had done something wrong but could not figure out what.

I think I had been as close to starting a riot as I ever would. Still wondering what all that had been about, I picked up the rope tail that was tied to a leather bucket, which had been folded and stored behind the stringer.

The other buckets were in use. We mixed the food in one, and the other was used in the for'ard accommodation for natural body functions, then the contents were tipped over the side. This one was to come in very handy, filling it with sea water to wash ourselves down.

I thought that a leather bucket in a small boat was a smart idea. When you are finished with it, you just fold it up and stash it in any corner out of the way. Compared to an ordinary bucket which takes up space and keeps rolling about unless stowed properly.

Sitting back at the tiller, Luc and Poi explained to me about the old man and his stick. They told me that the stick was some kind of religious symbol made out of a special type of wood. They believed that to be touched by it was a means to ward off evil spirits and bring good luck. The old man had carried the stick with him all his life and was only trying to help and protect me the only way he knew how. By touching me with it.

I felt a proper bastard, when I thought of how quickly

I was prepared to throw the old man's stick over the side because of my ignorance. I really felt low.

To try and make amends, I punctured two holes in a tin of condensed milk and gave it to him in the hold, along with a tin of orange juice. He drank half the tin of milk in one go, sucking it through the holes, his eyes sparkling like a child's, with the sweet taste.

He then started muttering some sort of ritual, touching me on the head, shoulders, arms and legs with the stick, until finally with a big grin he touched my private parts with it, muttering louder.

A bit taken aback, I went aft and asked Luc what the hell all that was about! In his broken English he made me understand that I had received some sort of major blessing, ending with the touching of my private parts with the stick. This was a separate blessing for me, to have many sons like myself, to make the world a kinder place. That old man sure knew how to make a person feel very humble and unassuming.

That afternoon we steamed for half an hour through a large shoal of fish. We had been seeing dolphins and all types of seabirds for the last two days, and even steamed through a mass of turtles that looked like helmets dotted all over the calm sea.

The only time we stopped seeing any natural life, which was abundant all over, was when the sea seemed to boil and bubble yesterday.

It is very seldom that we see much wildlife on the ship

except an odd whale which wanders about, contentedly grazing and browsing round the oceans, and the usual birds, which differ in the northern and southern hemispheres. I think that the noise of such a large mass of steel passing through the water frightens everything away long before we reach the area.

We topped up the fuel tank again, using up the second drum of diesel and checked the engine to make sure everything was secure before nightfall.

In the late afternoon the wind started to fade away, leaving a marked difference in our speed. About an hour later it dropped all together leaving the sea unruffled.

Thinking about the sail, which I thought would now be acting as a break holding us back, I called to Luc and Poi to lower it. As they went up the deck to lower it, Carp shouted in his own language and caught the lower batten swinging the sail round the mast, featuring it in a fore and aft position so as not to cause any drag as the boat chugged along, back down to three to four knots. The more I saw of the sail, the more I realised how clever the design had been developed over the years, making life easier, doing away with having to haul it up and down the mast for tacking.

After the sail was feathered, for want of a better word, I was setting the lashing on the tiller, when I noticed that they had all gathered in the hold again and were deep in discussion, glancing my way now and then nodding and smiling.

"Oh, oh. There's something brewing," I thought. "What now?" As I was preparing myself for another dust-up, Luc came out of the hold and stood beside me not saying a word. Then Poi came out carrying what I thought was a bundle of cloth, until he stood in front of me and lifted the cover off his baby daughter's face.

He then pointed to me saying, "Kinee" and then at the baby saying, "Kinee, Kinee." I couldn't understand what he was on about until Luc explained after a fashion that he wanted to name his daughter after me. I took it all as a big joke and managed to explain that 'Kinee', as it sounded, was a boy's name not a girl's.

He looked at me a while, his mind working in overtime trying to work out what I had said, and then he thrust the baby at me, making me hold it while he removed the rest of the covering. He and Luc kept nodding and smiling, saying together, "You name, you name."

As I looked past him towards the hold I could see the heads and shoulders of the women and the old man all looking at me, nodding and smiling, waiting for me to say something.

It is strange the things that go through a person's mind when they are in a difficult situation. All of a sudden I thought of one of the hills at home, and with tears in my eyes I looked at the baby, which seemed so small, and said in Gaelic, "Tha i cho beag 's a tha Eitseal mòr," which translated meant, "She is as small, as Eitseal is big."

When they asked me what I had said, I tried to explain, telling them that Eitseal was a hill in Lewis. But Luc and Poi seemed to grasp the word Eitseal, repeating it over and over, pronouncing it as Ayal, until Poi started nodding and turning with the baby. He held it up to the rest shouting, "Ayal, Ayal."

They all started singing and clapping. The old man scrambled out of the hold and placed his stick on Poi's head, and then all over the baby, muttering in a sing-song voice some sort of rhyme, of which the only word that I could understand was Ayal, which was being referred to quite often.

They all seemed quite happy, except me. When I thought of Eitseal and home, I could not stop crying for a while with a terrible bout of homesickness. I soon got over this when Poi came and asked me to write his daughter's name and where she was born, on the deck with a charcoal stick that he gave me.

Not sure what to do, I had to think about, and work out, the distance from Singapore to where I first boarded the boat. All I could do was work out fifteen hours at twelve knots, the speed of my ship, which worked roughly, knots to miles, at about two hundred and a bit miles.

I wrote on the deck below the gunnel on the port side aft, with the charcoal stick:

"Ayal, daughter of Poi born approx 200 miles N by E of Singapore. Very weak. I don't think she will survive. K.M.D. E.D.H."

Such a cruel waste.

When I had finished, I threw the stick down on the deck and went back to sit by the tiller, feeling very depressed at not being able to do more.

After a while moping about, I managed to shake off my depression and fix the navigation lights which gave off a good green and red glow.

Looking round, I could see ships' lights on both sides of us in the distance, so I tried to make Luc and Poi understand what green and red lights meant, especially with a white one in between them.

After about half an hour of futile, frustrating tuition, I had to give up because they just didn't seem to be able to grasp the navigation systems of ships at sea. So I told them to take turn about up in the bow, more than anything to get them out of my hair, and to let me know if they saw any kind of light ahead of us, as I couldn't see over the stem from my position at the tiller.

After a few minutes, Poi started shouting from the bow, "You see, you see."

When I went up to where he was in the bow, he was pointing to a ship's light away on the horizon on the port side, steaming in the opposite direction, miles away from us.

I was very tired by now, and had just reached the tiller when he started shouting again, "You see, you see." Up to the bow again, where this time he is pointing to a fishing boat, the same distance away on the starboard side. In the end I gave up, and told him to come back down to the tiller with me.

I couldn't dare to go to sleep, so I slowed the engine down to about half-speed and every twenty minutes or so I swerved to port and then to starboard, making sure the horizon ahead was clear of shipping.

Before dark, I had cleaned out the bucket that was used for natural functions in the accommodation, and had soaked some rags in diesel fuel, lighting them with my lighter when I needed to check the compass, after swerving from port to starboard.

Yesterday I had started to have tremors in my hands off and on, which gradually grew worse until now. They were constantly shaking, which I put down to the lack of sleep. I also noticed that my head was beginning to tremble and shake uncontrollably for periods of fifteen to thirty minutes at a time. I was beginning to get a bad dose of the shakes.

Poi had been with me at the tiller for most of the night, and some time in the early hours of the morning Luc came running down the deck waving his arms and shouting, "Come look see, come look see. You quick, you quick."

When I didn't take any notice of him, he started chattering to Poi, pulling him towards the bow. They were gone for about a minute, and I could hear their raised voices excitedly discussing something up in the bow.

Then they both came out of the darkness at me, shouting, "Look see, look see. You come," and started to pull me towards the bow. When I went with them to the bow, they were pointing at a faint orange glow in the sky, low on the horizon, which was the glow given off by a town or city at night. They kept pointing and repeating, "Maya, Maya." I told them that I did not know, and tried to explain that the glow could be anything from fifty to one hundred miles away.

When I went back to the tiller, my hands were shaking so much that I had difficulty opening the lashing. So I left it on, and corrected the course by pushing against it, stretching the rope.

As dawn came, the tension of steaming in the darkness seemed to leave me, easing my shakes enough for me to hold a bowl of water without spilling it, and to roll a cigarette. About an hour after dawn the mist started to rise again reducing visibility to about half a mile.

Food and water was being passed around and I gave another two omnopon tablets to the women, along with sulpha powder for the injured woman.

I had increased our speed back to our usual three to four knots and taken the lashing off the tiller. Carp, who had been trying to feed the man with the bulging eyes, was walking back down the deck shaking his head and telling Luc and Poi, who were standing beside me, that he could not even get him to take water today.

As they were talking amongst themselves, the man

with the bulging eyes rose and made three steps, the third and final step over the gunnel and into the sea. Without looking either left or right, looking straight ahead, he stepped over the side as if he were just stepping off the pavement.

I put the boat hard a-starboard so as to swing the stern and propeller away from him, slamming the throttle down and kicking the gear-lever into neutral at the same time. I was looking slightly to astern to the mark where he had gone down, so that I could come round and pick him up, when Luc said, "You leave. Him happy now. No more sore." While Luc was saying this to me, Poi pushed the gear-lever into ahead and made signs for me to go back to the tiller.

I had one last look around, and knew that they were right. The man went straight down and did not come back to the surface.

When we were underway again the shakes came back tenfold. As I saw the man take his first step, the bandage or cloth came off his right foot, and I could see a blood clot where his small toe should have been. I could also see the bone of the next toe, where the flesh had been cut by the point of whatever had been used to cut off the outer toe. His suffering must have been unbearable.

I kept thinking why I didn't give him some omnopon. But I didn't know he was in such pain, as he never spoke or moaned. He didn't speak or make a sound all the time he was on the boat.

I can't understand why the others kept so quiet about him, and when I asked, they told me about the compound again and said pointing to their feet, "No sore, no sore." Then, touching their heads they said, "Sore here. Sore here," and pointing to the sea said, "No more sore. No more sore. Him happy now."

11

His death didn't seem to affect me so much as the shock of finding Shom's body on the fore-deck. The more I thought of how I threw his body over the side, the more my shaking increased.

My hands were shaking so much that there were tremors going down the tiller to the rudder, making it rattle on the pintles. I couldn't control my head which was now shaking so much that my neck was sore. I knew that it was all caused by the strain I had been under for the last two days, and the mounting tensions due to the lack of sleep.

As we were in amongst the shipping lanes, in poor visibility and land not too far away, I couldn't dare go to sleep.

So I thought of the benies in the first-aid chest, and knew that if there ever was a need for them, it was now.

Raking around in the chest, I found them in their sealed alloy tube. Breaking the seal, I counted six round yellow pills in the tube, a square of paper and a small pencil to record how the benzedrine had been used, also the reason for breaking the seal.

As I wasn't able to write with my shaking hands, I swallowed one pill, washing it down with some water.

I put the top back on the tube, and replaced it in the first-aid chest.

Sitting on my container, back at the tiller, I could feel the tiredness leaving me, and the shaking of my head easing off until it stopped after about five minutes.

Within fifteen minutes after taking the benie, my shakes had gone completely, leaving me feeling as if I had just woken up after a good night's sleep.

With the new lease of life I had acquired from the benie, I checked the engine, stern tube and bilge. I then filled the fuel tank with our last drum of diesel.

As I was checking the fresh water, which was down to about twelve gallons, I saw Poi crouching over the charcoal writing that I had written on the deck for him.

When I had finished making sure that everyone was as comfortable as they could be, I checked the sail. It was still feathered, in case a sudden gust of wind came, which I doubted, as we were in the mist and haze you usually get about forty odd miles out from land. After I had done all that I could think of, I went back to the tiller and sat watching Poi.

Poi, a determined man, determined that there would be some kind of permanent record kept of his daughter's birth, the small baby daughter that he loved so much, for such a short time. He was carving the charcoal writing on the deck with his knife. Carving out each letter I had drawn on the planks.

I was a bit worried about how he would react when he

114

came to the part about her being weak and not going to survive. But I needn't have worried. As he finished carving, I knew that he didn't understand, for he even carved out the smudge the charcoal stick left on the deck where I threw it down after I had finished writing with it.

That night, darkness fell very quick, due to the mist. Even with the lights on, I was still very worried about other ships and fishing boats, most of which didn't have radar. Also, I wanted to keep away from land until daylight enabled us to see where we were going.

So, I shut the throttle down until the engine was ticking over in gear at its minimum speed, which gave us about half a knot. Poi and Carp were on the fore-deck as lookouts, their heads swivelling back and fore and up and down, peering into the darkness and mist.

Twice during the night we heard the sound of engines passing close to us. One of them was the heavy throb of a ship's engines, and the other was the higher revving engine of a fishing boat.

After a long night, when dawn finally came we still couldn't see land. The mist and haze hadn't cleared. Visibility was the same as yesterday, about half a mile. I knew that we were close to land, and didn't want to spend another night at sea, so I pulled the throttle up to maximum speed, come what may.

As we ploughed our way through the mist, about mid morning we could hear the sound of an aircraft engine, which seemed to be coming from the mist ahead. I didn't take much notice of it, until I saw a massive plane with four huge spinning propellers coming out of the mist ahead of us, at what I thought was about fifty feet above the water.

It flew down our port side with a thunderous ear-splitting roar, so low that the air wash of the propellers was ruffling the sea behind it. As it passed us, a blast of wind caught our sail heeling us over, leaving us rocking as it passed astern of us.

Luc and Poi who had been on the fore-deck dived in to the hold and were huddled with the rest, terrified on the floorboards. As I watched, the plane climbed and started to circle back, lining up on us. This time it was far higher, with the flaps underneath it open, and the undercarriage down.

I remember thinking that, with the mist, we must have steamed into a bay that had an airfield closeby, and that the plane was preparing to land.

So, thinking that we were going to go aground or hit the shore, I slammed the throttle down and put the engine into neutral. It was some months later I found out that when a pilot wants to fly slower, he lowers the undercarriage so as it will act as air-brakes.

It flew directly over the top of us, retracting its wheels as it started to climb, disappearing into the mist again. I put the engine back into gear and set the throttle at half-speed, the compass on south by west.

The people in the hold had got over their fright and were in deep discussion, no doubt wondering what was going to happen to them when they got ashore.

12

I was sitting at the tiller, trying to roll a cigarette with difficulty as my hands had started to shake again, when Luc and Poi came out of the hold. As they came towards me I could see that Luc was carrying a small tobacco sized box. They both sat down cross-legged on the deck in front of me, and placed the box on the deck between us.

Luc spoke to Poi in his own language and, reaching over, opened the hinged lid on the box and took out three small objects, which were individually wrapped in bits of cloth. As he placed them on the deck in front of me he said, "You take, you take, we go, you finish, you go ship."

I unwrapped the first object and it looked to me like a shiny brass bar, about six inches long by half an inch wide, by maybe a quarter of an inch thick, with ten square segments like a strip of chocolate bar. When I unwrapped the others, they were identical.

It took me a long while to realise that what I had at first thought were some kind of brass trinkets, were in fact three small bars of gold, which they were giving to me.

The only gold I had ever seen before was either in

rings or doubtful watches. I knew I could not take them.

The poor people aboard had suffered all kinds of hardships and horrors, just to be able to stay alive and try to live in peace. They would need everything they had, to start a new life wherever they ended up.

I wrapped the bars up in their bits of cloth and, shaking my head, handed them back to Luc. He placed them back on the deck in front of me and pointing to each one he said. "Day one, day two, day three," meaning he was wanting to give me one bar for each day I had been with them aboard the boat. When I shook my head again, and pushed the bars back, he took another bar from the box thinking there wasn't enough, and that I was wanting more.

This went on for some time, until in the end I reached over to take the box. But as I tried to pull it away, Luc held on to it, until Poi spoke to him. Whatever Poi said, I don't know, but Luc reluctantly let me have the box and as I pulled it over to me I could see another four bars inside it.

They had thought that I was going to take all of it and it was a pleasure to see the dejected look on their faces change to a look of puzzlement and then amazement as I placed all the bars back in the box and pushed it back over to them, saying, "You keep, you keep."

Having spent weeks hiding from robbers and bandits, they couldn't understand why I didn't want to take their prized possessions. I wouldn't have known what to do with it anyway. They went back into the hold, and from the looks I was getting, they were obviously telling the rest about the fool at the tiller.

I couldn't care less. I was slowly losing interest in all around me. The shakes had returned with a vengeance. I was like an old man with palsy, shaking so much that I couldn't sit on my container beside the tiller. All I wanted to do was sleep.

About two hours after the plane flew over us, I could hear the sound of powerful engines in the mist. As they grew louder, a naval craft of about eighty feet long, bristling with guns and radars whizzing round on every corner, appeared out of the mist ahead of us, doing about thirty knots.

He swept down our starboard side in a spray of foam and bow-wave, slowing down and swinging round our stern, to come up on our port side, stopping alongside and shouting in English for us to heave to. I pushed the throttle down and took her out of gear, and as we were slowing down, the navy launch came in alongside, bumping on her fenders.

Two uniformed crew jumped aboard with ropes and made us fast fore and aft. They then passed a heavy rope from her quarter making it fast to our mid-ships, and started to tow us, lashed alongside, at what I was sure was nearly ten knots. It wasn't the first time they had done this. They knew exactly where to tie the ropes, and the safest maximum speed to steam at.

They didn't speak to any of us, and the two sailors who jumped aboard with the ropes returned silently to their own boat, taking up their stations fore and aft.

13

We were towed along for about an hour, then slowed down and stopped when what looked like a harbour tug appeared from the direction of land.

It steamed down our port side round our stern and made fast to our starboard side, spewing out officials, some in uniforms and others in civilian dress.

Sitting on my container, I could see the bland expressionless faces of Luc and Poi waiting patiently, willing to accept whatever the future held for them and their families.

After a while I heard a distant plummy voice speaking to me, and I had to force myself to drag my eyes away from those in the hold, to turn round and see a clean, spotless American or Canadian officer standing beside me.

As I looked at him, trying to make up my mind whether to hit him or shake his hand, he held up a sheet of paper and asked, "Is your name Macdonald?" I managed to whisper, "Yes." Then the tears came and I broke down completely.

He signalled to two sailors on the patrol boat who came aboard, and with one on each side supporting me, they helped me across the deck and aboard their own boat.

Standing on the side deck of the patrol boat, I looked down through my tears at the expressionless faces of the brave people who I had got to know so well in the last three days.

While I was wondering what was going to happen to them, and who was going to look after them now, the injured woman started speaking to Luc and Poi, the first words I heard her speak since I came aboard the boat. Whatever she said, Luc and Poi climbed out of the hold and helped her to her feet, supporting her.

As she stood facing me, she lifted her arm and waved to me, a gesture that must have cost her sorely and dearly in pain and effort. As she sagged back, Luc and Poi lowered her gently to the deck where an officer with a red cross badge on his shoulder started to attend to her. That just finished me.

When another officer with a red cross on his jacket said that I would have to go with him, I felt so ashamed. I was blubbering like a child, and through my sobs all I could think of was the bosun's last words, that he wanted the lifeboat compass back.

I seemed to cling on to this, repeating "compass," "compass," over and over again, until they took me into the accommodation and stretched me out on a bed in what looked to be a small hospital.

A man dressed in casual kind of slept-in looking clothes asked me if I had taken any drugs, and I managed to tell him that I had taken one benzedrine pill yesterday.

He immediately spoke to one of the sailors, and I heard the first-aid chest being mentioned. Then the sailor disappeared for about fifteen minutes.

When he came back, the two of them had a discussion in the doorway for a moment or two and then he told me that everything was going to be fine, that they had checked the first-aid chest, and that he was now going to give me an injection to make me sleep. I remember feeling the needle going into my arm, and nothing else.

14

My first recollection is of waking up with a terrible thirst, and feeling cold. I thought that we had docked and tied up, and that I was still aboard my ship, because there wasn't any movement or motion, and I could hear the sound of what I thought were the shore generators in the engine room.

I lay in my bunk for a minute or two, until I realised that something was not quite right. I couldn't hear the banging and thumping of dockers working on the deck above, and I wasn't getting any vibrations through the bulkhead from the engine room.

I sat up with a start, wondering where the hell the pyjamas I was wearing came from, and who had put them on me. I then realised that I wasn't on a ship but in a three-quarter width bed, covered with white sheets in a white room, that measured about twenty feet by fifteen feet. There was a toilet and wash hand basin in the corner. Above it, a rail had been fixed to the ceiling for hanging a curtain or screen for privacy, which had been removed.

A tubular framed chair and table, with a jug of water and a bottle of barley water, stood in the other corner. The noise which I thought had been the engine room generators was coming from an air-conditioning unit that was purring away in the wall beside the only window, which had square steel mesh-sheeting bolted to it from the outside. All I could see through the window was trees and bushes, that were so close to the window they were blocking out most of the light.

With my thirst, I gulped down the jug of water and instantly felt as if my bladder was going to burst. So, as I was peeing into the toilet, wondering if I was ever going to stop, the door opened and a man with a white coat over some kind of uniform entered. He said that he was a Canadian doctor working for the Red Cross, and when I asked his name he was very evasive, asking me instead how I was.

By this time, I had finished peeing and was a bit embarrassed. All I could think of to ask him was, "Why isn't there a screen round the toilet?"

He answered me saying, "All the screens have been removed because the people who arrive here have to be under constant surveillance for the first forty eight hours."

I asked him why, and he said, "Most of those sent here are not physically ill but mentally ill. Their mental illness has been brought on by the horrific sights they have witnessed and the horrors that have been committed against them. Some of them will never get better, they will spend the rest of their lives, such as it is, somewhere, cowering in the corner of a padded room, trying to squeeze themselves through the walls. Others recover after a period of time. Some, as you, a lot quicker."

When I asked him how he knew I was better, he told me to go to the door and look out. I went to the door, opened it, and looking out I could hear what sounded to me like human voices, unlike anything I had ever heard before, or ever want to hear again.

The corridor was running the full length of the building, with four other doors to my right and three to my left. There was also a man in a short white jacket, who looked like a native orderly, sitting in a chair placed in such a position that he could watch all eight doors.

When I went back into the room, the doctor was sitting in the chair beside the table. He asked me what I had seen, so I told him about the other rooms and the orderly. He then told me that this was how he knew I was better and recovering.

I asked him, "How?" He said that I had slept for twenty four hours, considering that the injection I had been given by the doctor on the patrol boat was only meant to knock me out for two hours. "You did have a minor breakdown, but it was mostly due to exhaustion and stress. The rest, you seem to have shrugged off remarkably well. Your first question to me was to ask my name, and for a screen round the toilet."

"The people who end up here couldn't care less about my name, or being embarrassed by their natural functions. They would never go to the door as you just have. All they want to do is crouch in a dark corner of the room or lie whimpering on the bed until relief is given to them with drugs, to ease the pain in their minds with the comfort of sleep. They are even terrified of the door opening. That is why, if you look at the door, you will see a spy-hole. This allows the orderly to check the occupants of each room without having to open the doors."

Sitting on the bed in somebody else's pyjamas, wondering where I was, I asked him and he told me that it wasn't important. The important thing was for me to be well enough to join my ship tomorrow.

When I asked him about the others that had been on the boat with me, he said that they were being well looked after, and that they were going to make a full recovery, including the baby and the injured woman.

As soon as I started talking and thinking about those who had been with me, it all started flooding back to me and my head and hands began to shake again. I asked him about the compass, and he said that a number of items had been stored in a building for me, including the compass.

The captain of my ship had informed the authorities when they docked. The aeroplane spotted us about two miles off the Malayan coast, nine miles to the north west of Singapore. When the pilot radioed our position back to his base, they informed the Singapore navy, who sent out a patrol boat, followed by the harbour tug.

Luc and Poi had been interned with their families in a refugee camp. When I asked him where the camp was, all he would tell me was that they were being well looked after, changing the conversation by calling the orderly in and telling him to refill the water jug.

When the orderly returned with the fresh water, he gave a small round box of pills to the doctor, and said that arrangements to return me to the ship had been made. I would be returning at seven a.m. tomorrow. By now my hands were shaking quite violently and the doctor told me to go back to bed, giving me one of the pills out of the box to help me sleep, which I washed down with half the jug of water.

Early the next morning I was woken by a different orderly and he had put my clothes, such as they were, which had been washed and pressed, in a neat pile on the table. He gave me tea and some kind of porridge on a wooden tray, which I wolfed down without tasting, in my desperation to get out of that place of lost souls and anguish.

15

When we went outside, there was a badly dented Volkswagen van that had its windows painted out, standing in front of the door.

The orderly I had met the day before was sitting in the driver's seat, and the doctor in the passenger seat. Two other men came out of what looked like a store-room carrying the lifeboat first-aid chest between them, with my lifejacket, two buckets, a deck-broom and the compass balanced on top.

As they were sliding it into the van, I noticed a long, sharp pointed iron spike, with a handle at one end lying on top of the chest between the two buckets. I picked the spike off the chest and told the orderly that it didn't belong to me, and he said, "One of the refugees on the boat put it on the chest, and told us to give it to you, so as you would always remember."

Thinking that it was all a bit strange, I picked the spike up and asked him what it was. He replied saying, "I think that it's an old First World War French bayonet."

The shock when I realised that it was the bayonet that had been used on the poor injured woman on the boat made me slump against the van, dropping the bayonet in the dust, as if it was red hot. I told them that I didn't want anything to do with it, and clambered into the back of the van, leaving the bayonet lying on the road, wishing that I had never seen it.

A partition had been placed behind the driver and passenger seats, stopping me seeing out the front. The orderly in the back with me just shrugged his shoulders when I asked him why I wasn't allowed to see out, or to know where I was.

The only complaint I had was when I asked him, "How far are we from the sea, and what direction is the sea in?" His answer was, "That doesn't concern you. We are taking you back to your ship, so leave it at that." I felt like hitting him, the ignorant man. What else was a seaman, stuck in what seemed to be the middle of a jungle, going to ask?

We drove slowly for about an hour, on a very rough track or road. Then we stopped for about a minute or two at what I think was a check point, as I could hear someone talking to the driver, but I couldn't make out what they were saying because of the noise the engine was making in the back of the van.

When we moved off again, we went over a large bump on the road as if it was some kind of ramp, and drove for about an hour and a half on a smooth tarred road. We started to slow down, and I could tell that we were entering a town or large village because I could hear other traffic passing, horns blowing and the nearly continuous ringing of bicycle bells, the van, stopping and turning round corners, and giving way to other traffic.

I was getting fed-up, and had given up trying to make conversation with the orderly or nurse, or whatever he was.

When I heard the sound of a ship's siren blowing twice and then three times, I knew that we were close to the docks, as that was the sure sound of a ship manoeuvring with tugs. After about another ten minutes, crawling through noise and bustle, the van stopped and the side doors opened.

We had stopped beside my ship, at the bottom of the gangway. I made a dive to get out of the van but the orderly grabbed me and held me back. The doctor then came into the back of the van and sat down on the bench opposite me, signalling to the orderly to leave, and waiting for him to close the doors behind him.

He said that I had been very lucky, and obviously, like most in the western world, had never experienced the horror and residues of distant wars in countries where law and order has broken down and ceased to exist; where man can do as he pleases with no fear of repercussions. He continued, "Any law or order, no matter how oppressive or unjust it seems at the time, is far better than to allow man to roam freely, unshackled, performing his viciousness at will against his fellow man."

"What is horror and cruelty to you and others like you, who have led a relatively sheltered life, is an everyday occurrence, and so common to others, that I am sad to say they think nothing of it.

"Your problem was caused by exhaustion, and experiencing for the first time what man can do to man. Also with the strain of the last few days, when it was over, your mind decided that it had enough, shutting itself down for a rest, using crying as a relief valve. You have nothing to be ashamed of, as it is all quite normal and natural."

I was only half listening to him, as all I wanted to do was get out of the van, back aboard my ship and as far away as possible. He told me not to take any of the pills unless I thought I really needed them.

As I shook his hand, thanking him for everything and saying goodbye, he said, "And for Christ's sakes, think long and hard before you ever do anything like that again!"

I know that he was right, because somehow or other I had suffered in my sub-conscious for those three days and nights - the pain and terror, the apprehensions and degradation, of these gentle desperate people.

16

When I went back aboard the ship, all my gear had been shifted out of my cabin, which I shared with another seaman, and put into the day-worker's cabin, who had been shifted into my berth.

The day-worker meant just that he didn't have any watch-keeping duties to do, he just worked shore hours, seven to five plus overtime. He was on standby in case any of the watch-keepers took sick, also taking the first fire and gangway watch in port.

I got the usual good-natured banter and innuendos from the crew about what was called my escapade, and was trying to decide whether to go ashore for a drink with them, or to turn in, when the bosun knocked on my cabin door and waited to be asked in.

I thought that either the captain or the doctor had been having a word with him. Before, when he used to come to a cabin looking for you, he would bellow, "Are you in there?" And the door would burst open. This time, he waited for me to shout, "Come in!" and even then I had to open the door for him.

When he came into the cabin, he spoke to me as if I was a ten year old child, telling me that I had been put on light duties for a week, and if I needed anything whatsoever, his words, to let him know.

As he was talking to me, I was puzzled why he had kept one hand behind his back, until he made to leave, then he said, "Oh! I nearly forgot," and taking his hand from behind his back, he gave me six tins of beer, and said, "I thought you would want this, seeing you never got a chance to go ashore."

I thanked him, and as he was stepping out into the alleyway he mumbled over his shoulder, "It's good to have you back. We're sailing at 1700hrs tomorrow."

When he left, I was wondering what he meant by that, with the memory of the swipe I gave him five days ago still fresh in my mind. That was it! My mind was made up.

I took the beer down to the mess-room, where it disappeared amongst nine of us in about ten seconds. Then we all headed for the first shebeen at the dock gates.

We were in the process of getting roaring drunk, when about twenty to thirty Royal Navy sailors from the navy base, dressed and polished in immaculately pressed uniforms, seemed to pour in the door.

I was reasonably clean. but had a seven day growth of beard. The rest of the crew had spent the day stripping down the jumbo derrick, and were covered in grease from the tackles and sheaves. The only part of them that was clean was their hands which had been washed, leaving a tide mark on their wrists.

Those who have frequented shebeens will know that they are the same all over. You can only buy bottled beer, which is sold out of large chiller chests over a bar counter made out of planks nailed with six inch spikes, sometimes to the trunk of a tree or any other heavy bulk of timber. The seats are made out of beer-crates, the tables two beer-crates one on top of the other, with a square of plywood nailed on top, and of course the compulsory juke box, thumping away in its wire-mesh cage behind the bar.

We watched them from our end of the bar, buying three bottles of beer at a time, and drinking them down, one after another. This went on for over an hour, until one of the sailors called us a bunch of dirty bumboat ballast.

As those things happen, nobody really knows who strikes the first blow. The place erupted into a fearful furore, beer-crates and bottles flying through the air, with a seething mass grappling and swinging at each other.

Coincidence is a strange thing. As I was rolling about on the floor, trying to strangle one of the sailors with his uniform collar, which I had swung round to pin his arm that held a broken bottle against the side of his head, I knew that I was choking him. But I also knew that if I eased off he would stick me in the face with the jagged glass.

We had reached a bit of a stalemate, until he managed to gasp out, "I know you. You're the guy on the boat we were looking for." It took me a moment to register, but when I looked closer I recognised him as the bow-man on the patrol boat.

Thinking of all the sailors in the shebeen, how the hell did I end up trying to strangle the only one who knew me? Still locked in stalemate on the floor, I said, "Fuck this. Come on and I'll buy you a beer." He gasped out, "Aye," and dropped the broken bottle.

I let go of his collar, and we both went on our hands and knees through the melee, which had now been joined by four native dock police, in their baggy calf-length shorts, who were standing in a group close to the door, not sure where to start, or what to do.

We crawled underneath the bar counter and sat on the floor out of harm's way, with our backs propped against one of the beer chillers. I had dropped the equivalent of three pounds into the chiller amongst the beer bottles, so we just sat yarning, helping ourselves as required.

After a while, we decided to shift to another shebeen up the road as the one we were in was getting a bit heavy. We had just arrived when a swarm of MPs and civilian police descended on what was left of our last residents.

Watching from a distance, the place seemed to explode. We saw sailors and seamen come through the windows, doors and walls, and two in separate places escaping through the roof. We watched for a short time until an MP, who had been left to guard the van, started to take an unhealthy interest in us.

Before he could make up his mind whether to leave his van and come over to question us, we ran round the corner and into the shebeen by a side door.

This shebeen was empty, as all the customers had left to watch the fight between the MPs and the sailors, who had now been joined by a crowd of dockers. We sat in the peace and quiet for a while, drinking beer, until my new found drinking pal decided to go off with one of the women in the bar. She was a little over five foot high and about a fathom wide, and there was never a truer phrase than blind drunk.

I had another beer by myself and, deciding that I had enough, made my way back to the ship, passing the first shebeen with a wide swerve as now there was a large bus and four more navy vans parked outside it.

When I got aboard the ship, I was very surprised to see that nearly all the crew had managed to get back aboard in one piece. All of them looked the worse for wear, with cuts, scratches and a lot of heavy bruising, feeling a bit sorry for themselves but still able to move around.

When we turned-to the next morning to start clearing away and battening-down to go to sea on the evening tide, the deck crew worked as if in slow motion, with stiff joints and aches and pains.

There was a single leg of a navy uniform bell bottom trouser flying like a flag from the top jib of one of the dock cranes. Nobody knew who put it there, but everybody was sure that it belonged to one of the MPs.

We sailed that night for Brisbane, and now being a day worker, I turned-in about eleven, and had a good night's sleep. I turned-to next morning at seven and the bosun gave me three new five gallon jerricans and took me up to the officers' accommodation into the captain's bathroom. He pointed at a bath full of cooking oil and said, "Fill the jerricans. Scrub the bath. I want it spotless. You've got until Brisbane!" Brisbane, I thought, that's nearly four days, no bother. I was wrong. I filled the jerricans with oil, and pulled the plug on the rest.

I then started scrubbing the bath with soogee, ajax and even neat tepol, but every time I ran the hot water a slick of oil floated to the surface. After spending the whole day scrubbing that bloody bath, in desperation I went aft to the lampy's locker and pinched about two pounds of caustic soda.

I dumped the lot into the bath, ran some water, and spread it around with a mop, until the head of the mop started to disintegrate. When I pulled the plug to let the water go, it had melted to a blob of black jelly on the end of its chain. The inside of the bath had a white matt finish on it, because the caustic soda had eaten away the enamel.

I cut and shaped another plug out of a small piece of dunnage that I found in the chippy's locker and painted it matt black. When I fitted it on the end of the chain, you couldn't tell the difference.

My only interruption was from the second officer who came in to collect a book for the captain. As he was speaking, he kept trying to hide his face from me, which he managed to do, until I saw his reflection in the bathroom mirror. His face and eyes were in an awful mess with bruises.

When the dust-up in the shebeen had been in full swing, he had stood in the doorway trying to do his officer bit. He was shouting at everybody to behave themselves, when someone hit him full in the face with a bag of frozen ice cubes.

We discharged and loaded in Brisbane and Melbourne, then headed for Panama, with an uneasy truce between me and the bosun. When we arrived in Bilbao, we had to anchor for eight hours, waiting our turn to go through the canal.

It doesn't matter how many times I have been through Panama, it still doesn't seem right. It is more of an uncanny sight, like something out of this world, to watch huge ocean-going ships creeping their way up a mountain, with the jungle on both sides of them.

The rest of the trip was reasonably routine except when the captain developed a bad case of dhobi-rash from the waist down, and gave his steward a roasting for not rinsing out his skivvies properly. It wasn't the steward's fault. I reckon that the captain's bits and bobs must have been tingling with the residue of the caustic soda I had left in his bath.

17

We docked in Liverpool, and were paying off the next day. The Captain sent word down that he wanted to see me. I thought, this was it; that he had found out about his bath. But no.

As I went into his office, a small cubby-hole beside his cabin, he told me to sit down. He then poured me a large rum, and gave me an envelope with two weeks pay in it.

When I asked him what the extra money was for, he said that he was sorry he had to log me a week's pay for being absent without leave, but he had to keep his books right. At the time we had come across the drifting refugees, he had been placed between two major decisions: "One, to take the refugees aboard would have made us and the Company responsible for them, which would have caused days or even weeks of delay with the red tape of bureaucracy and jumped-up officials with a rubber stamp in one hand and the other hand held out for bribes, before they stamp any bit of paper.

"Two, to make sure that they had provisions and that their boat was seaworthy, fit enough to continue, which wasn't the case. Your decision to go aboard with them solved that one. But I would not have allowed you to go if the weather hadn't been so good, or if the bosun or the chippy had given me an adverse report on the seaworthiness of the boat. As you will no doubt agree now, she was a fine craft, well built.

"As to the money, I have returned the week's pay that I logged you, and added another week as a token from the Company."

I was a bit taken aback at all this and couldn't think of anything to say, so I finished my rum and thanked him.

As I was leaving his office, he said that they would be heading out again in three weeks if I was interested. I told him that I wasn't sure of what I would be doing, and went down to the cabin for my bag, and to the gangway for the waiting taxi.

I was halfway down the gangway when I heard the bosun shouting at me from the boat-deck. I asked him what he wanted, and he said, "Phone the dock office when you're ready, and there will be a berth waiting here for you." I told him that I was going down to London, but that I would be spending a couple of days in Liverpool anyway.

I had just reached the bottom of the gangway when he shouted again, "By the way, do you know who was buggering about with my whistle?" When I said to him, "What whistle?" he glared at me and said, "You know damn fine. I was looking back at the overtime sheets and you were the only one around working up on the monkey island that day, so you must have seen somebody."

I replied, "Oh, that whistle! No, I didn't see anybody,

but we did notice that you weren't blowing it so much lately." He said something that sounded like "Hurrumph," and disappeared from the taffrail. I dived into the taxi and said to the driver, "Let's get the hell out of here before thon crusty bugger reaches the gangway."

I booked into the Seamen's Mission that night, and five days later found me steaming down St. George's channel, fully loaded, battening down and banging home the hatch wedges of number two hold with the chippy.

Scattering a cold lumpy hash of weather from the south west with Cork and Dungarven to starboard, setting a course for Curacao, Panama, then New Zealand and Australia, to get the first of the fruit season back to the UK.

I just couldn't settle ashore, and started wandering round the docks after two days in the city.

You may ask why I didn't sign back on to my last ship again. Well, I was mulling it over, having one or two pints in the Carradock in Bootle, and between the bosun's whistle and the Captain's bath, I came to the conclusion that I would lead a far calmer life of it by giving her a wide berth until things cooled off for a bit.

I also heard in one of the bars that two separate dress designers were bidding against each other for a dress that a Vietnamese man had given to an engineer. It seemed to be some sort of rare silk dress, much in demand in the West. The last I heard was that he had refused to sell it at a hundred and twenty pounds. A lot of money.

18

Aye, he sailed for a number of years after that. Sailing west until west turned into east and until east turned into west.

From the north to the ice in the south, carrying and delivering cargoes of nearly everything that is humanly possible for man to produce. From cargoes of all the latest household gadgets, that the housewife uses in her kitchen and doesn't give a second thought as to how they arrived there or where they came from, so long as she can buy them in a shop, and probably one of the cars which sits on her tarmac drive, plus the oil to make it go and the rubber for its tyres. To even crated complete houses, in kit form, from Canada to the States.

Most of the trade goods, imported and exported then from the UK, were carried from all over the world in British ships manned by British seamen whose motto was, "Never leave the ship until the ship leaves you."

Oh he ended up in a number of scrapes with a few close shaves, and then a year or two fishing, so as not to be away from home for months at a time.

Until, in the end, the love of a beautiful wife and two lovely daughters and the adoration of a wee devil of a boy, in whom he saw so much of himself, far outweighed his love for the sea.

19

Still sitting on the tree he had been cutting, the white-haired man shivered, but not with the cold. He nipped his half-smoked cigarette which had long since gone out, and shaking his head as if to clear some dark thoughts from his mind, he ground the cigarette-end into the damp peat moss, with the heel of his boot. He knew full well that he had knowingly broken the promise he made to himself over thirty years ago.

A promise not to tell a living soul what happened to him, because of the shame of breaking down in front of the people he had tried to help, and in front of the people who took them ashore. Also the shame of being logged a week's pay by his captain for being absent without leave.

The reason he broke his promise after all those years is because of his daughter's recurring illness, and his beautiful little granddaughter, to whom he has nothing left to give except his love and his story.

Picking up his saw, he stood up stiffly and turned to look at the long straight tree he had been working on, thinking, "Aye, as good a mast as you would need for any boat." If only he could afford one, not too big because of the cost to maintain her, but big enough to put a horizon behind him one more time.

Sighing deeply, he turned and started walking back to his van.